My HUSBAND Looks Better in Lingerie Than I Do....DAMN IT

by Bobbie Thompson

Dedicated to everyone who has a transgender person in their life.

Copyright © by Bobbie Thompson
My **HUSBAND** Looks Better in Lingerie
Than I Do ... DAMN IT
www.myhusbandlooksbetter.com

All rights reserved. Except as permitted under U.S Copyright Act of 1976, no part of this publication may be reproduced, distributed, or transmitted in any form or by any means without the prior written permission of the author/publisher.

ISBN 13: 978-0-9914753-0-8 (paperback)
InnerLight LLC first printing, February 2014

self published via
InnerLight LLC
PO Box 1332
Versailles, KY 40383

Cover by Jay Stoner

Printed in the United States of America

ACKNOWLEDGEMENTS

First and foremost I must express my gratitude and appreciation for my wonderful spouse, Alana Nicole Sholar, who has opened my heart, opened my eyes, and brought me life experiences I could never ever have imagined possible.

Also, I want to thank the hundreds of transgender friends I have made, both in person and through social media, who have taught me first hand so very much about the varied experiences of persons in the transgender population.

And, I want to thank those friends, too numerous to mention, but you know who you are, that helped me by proofreading my manuscript and graciously offering suggestions and recommendations to improve my writing.

Author's Note: Some names have been changed in this memoir in respect for the privacy of the individuals involved.

INTRODUCTION

Those friggen names and pronouns! Some languages don't have gender distinctions in personal pronouns. I wish that were true for English. My normal every-day life experience is being married to a transgender person – someone I knew for nearly 30 years as Alan, as he or him, long before I ever became aware of Alana, as she or her. I still mix names and pronouns when I'm speaking to or about my spouse – and sometimes all in the same sentence.

I've come to the conclusion that when I use the name 'Alan' or 'Alana' it's always based on **MY** perspective of who *I'm* talking to or about and what gender 'I'm' identifying him or her as based on what *'I'm'* seeing, saying, or remembering. The gender changes, but the person never changes ... it's only my perspective that can change and after knowing the person in one gender for 30+ years, changing my perspective to another gender did not, and will not, come quickly. Just like Alana, I, too, am in a stage of transition ... only I am attempting to transition my brain to a different perspective, a different understanding of my spouse from the perspective I've had for decades.

No matter what I see or say, it's always based on what my brain tells me I see – or recognize – or perceive – the way my brain tells me to identify or define what I'm looking at. And I've come to realize that's the way it works for everyone. One can only speak from their own perspective – their own point of view – their own understanding – their own seeing. And one's perspective is always based on their experiences. No two people can have the same perspectives or understandings because no two people have the same experiences in life.

I don't have the same difficulty with using the correct name or pronoun when I meet other transgender persons. When I meet others, I'm introduced to them by the name they use based on the gender they're presenting – same with pronouns, for example: if the person is presenting as male, then I say he/him; if they are presenting as female I say she/her. Most of the time, I'm only aware of the name they use while presenting in that gender – so I don't experience the same difficulty with names and pronouns as I do when it comes to my spouse. I'm sure the difficulty arises from having known Alan for nearly 30 years before becoming aware of Alana, then trying to change my perspective to see, or recognize, or identify a different gender.

There are many instances in this writing, and my everyday living, where I begin the sentence by saying Alan then by sentence end, I'm saying Alana – or vice versa. That's how quickly my brain switches from perceiving a male to perceiving a female and sometimes right back again. Much of my seeing both male and female comes from knowing my spouse as a male for so many years before ever becoming aware of the word transgender.

Alan's name was legally changed to Alana in 2005, over a year before I saw 'her' for the first time. We were married in 2008, therefore, I married Alana. When my spouse and I meet someone new the name used for introduction is always Alana – but, because the person meeting Alana often perceives a male, they will sometimes refer to Alana as he or him. Again, they are only speaking from their perspective and understanding. Of course, much of their perspective is based on the fact that during her present stage of transition, Alana lives life 'hung in the middle' of two genders.

I believe sharing this information in this introduction will help clarify, thereby eliminate some confusion as to how I've used Alan/Alana, he/she, and him/her throughout the telling of 'my side' of our story. To get Alana's side, you'll have to read Alana's memoir, "*Hung in the Middle: A Journey of Gender Discovery.*" (www.hunginthemiddle.com)

Names and pronouns are a problem within themselves, but they're nothing compared to using and understanding various terms or vocabulary specific to being transgender. I've found that no matter what words I use, there will be someone who doesn't like it said 'that way' and will quickly let me know they are offended by my choice of words. Therefore, I'd like to point out this writing comes from what I know, what I've learned since becoming aware of transgender persons in 2006 ... not a very long time ago. As time progresses, I learn new terms and vocabulary that some consider more 'politically correct,' and should be used in place of many of the terms I learned initially. My vocabulary changes as my story progresses. However, in relaying my story and my understanding correctly, the words I use are the words I knew when expressing my experiences during particular time periods. The real kicker is, THE WORDS KEEP CHANGING, and I assume they always will since the only constant in life is change.

I've also included in this writing some of my personal life experiences during times when Alan/Alana wasn't in the picture. Much of this includes my experience with 'Little Redneck' as well as things I consider to be of a spiritual nature. I felt it necessary to include this information because it is these experiences and their coming together that forms my way of 'BE-ing' – in other words, it took ALL of these experiences to make me who I am – and are the basis for my understanding and perception of all things.

We are all who we are and perceive or understand things the way we do based on the culmination of our own experiences. We can think we know all there is to know about something, but we can have no real knowledge of anything until we have the experience of it. And even when it is our experience, ours is always different from any other experience, which gives each individual unique understanding of their experience, no matter how much our experiences may be similar to others.

For example, before I lost over 100 pounds, people would often say to me, "If you lose weight you'll feel so much better, you'll have so much more energy." I'm intelligent enough to have some comprehension of what their words meant, however, I had no knowledge, no true understanding of the experiences of feeling better and having more energy until I lost the weight. That's when I was truly able to 'know' what they had been telling me all along. So, no matter how much you think you know, you can never really know it all. Reading what

I share in this writing may give you some insight to the transgender experience, but, unless it is your experience to have been born transgender, you cannot 'know' the experience. And if it is your experience to have been born transgender, you can only truly know your 'personal' experience, which is different from any other.

I share my experiences of being an 'outside looking in' member of the transgender community, however, I don't claim to 'know' the experience of being transgender – and every person's life experience is different, period. People may, or may not, agree with my point of view on things I talk about in this writing. Some, based on their understanding, may believe I am 'right on' while others may believe I am 'dead wrong' in how I feel, or the choices I make, or the words I use. Either opinion is OK, because the feelings expressed and choices made and words used here are 'mine' and are perfect for me.

I don't write this to try and convince anyone that 'I'm right and you're wrong.' And, I don't write this to claim Alana's experience is the 'blueprint' for being transgender or mine is the 'blueprint' for being the spouse of a transwoman. I write this simply to share *MY* experiences in the hope that doing so can in some way help others having similar experiences and give some insight to those who have no idea what 'transgender' means. Yes, there have been times when I've said, "My spouse is transgender," and the person I'm talking to has immediately asked, "What's transgender?"

Bobbie Thompson
aka Alana's Spouse

PART 1
THE EXPERIENCE

01

YOU DON'T KNOW
WHAT YOU DON'T KNOW

"Hello," I said as I put the phone receiver to my ear.

"Hi, it's Alan," he said. "My mom told me your mom told her that you and your husband are getting a divorce."

"Yep," I answered, "he moved out."

"Well, I'm both sad and happy to hear that."

"Sad and happy? You're going to have to explain that one to me. I'm confused."

"I'm sad because I know you're going through rough times and I hate to see that."

I thought, *"Why do you hate to see me going through rough times, we've known one another for a long time, but we don't know one another that well."* But I never had the opportunity to ask that question because what he said next threw me for a loop.

"And I'm happy because I finally get the chance to tell you how attracted I've been to you all these years. I'd like for us to get together."

By 'get together' I knew exactly what he meant, but I couldn't imagine why he wanted us to 'get together.' I'm no raving beauty and am quite obese. I've always been a big girl. I remember back in first grade when the health

Alan

department came to school to give all us kids a checkup. I was the only first grader who already weighed 100 pounds. Then ten years later in my sophomore year in high school I was in art class with a bunch of other girls. We were to draw the items the art instructor had placed on our table, and one of the items was a measuring tape used in dressmaking. We decided we would all take our measurements – mine turned out to be 38-26-36 and I weighed 135 pounds. I hadn't gained a lot of weight over the 10 years, but to me I was still FAT. Those measurements and that weight might sound great to a lot of women, but I wasn't a woman, I was only 15 years old. Most of the other girls I saw every day walking the halls of the high school weighed somewhere between 95 and 110 pounds – I was 25 or more pounds heavier – and that's FAT.

During my sophomore year I met the only boy I ever dated in high school. I never ran around with anyone else, never attended a high school dance, never went to parties, and never made many friends. I just knew he and I would be together forever – he had all my attention. By the time we got married on August 18, 1972, the week before my senior year of high school began, my weight had already ballooned up to 175 pounds.

I'd already been married for four years when I turned 21 years old and gave birth to my son. From my perspective I'd accomplished everything I thought you were supposed to do in life – I was married, we had a child, my husband and I each had a job, we even had the little white house with the white picket fence - literally. It was in May 1976 when my son was born – lots of long haired hippies running around – but in my eyes, I was a long haired old married woman with a baby. I decided I needed to get my hair cut because I thought, *"old women don't look good with long hair."* I'd gained so much weight while pregnant that at age 21 my weight had already reached 250 pounds.

I have always had a warm, friendly, outgoing personality, but not much else going for me. By the time my husband and I separated in February 1994, after being married 22 years, the scales were up to 290 pounds and it scared me. Because I was so obese I couldn't imagine anyone ever wanting to 'get together' with me. That's why I was always so surprised by the number of conversations I'd had with married men since my husband and I had separated that included the words, "woe is me, my wife won't sleep with me any more so I was wondering if you and I could get together." I had very little respect for any man who would come on to me because I knew it couldn't possibly be me he wanted, it had to be just sex they were interested in. After all, what man in their right mind is really attracted to a woman who is only five foot two and tips the scales at 290 pounds? Conversations like these lead me to form my low opinion of a lot of men – which is: a man would come on to a dog if he thought it would get him laid.

I was of the old fashioned belief that when I said "I do" I became his and he became mine. Having an affair was never an option in my mind. I'm not sure if it was never an option because I'd been in church all my life and heard adultery preached against so often, or if I believed it was never an option because of my low self-esteem knowing no one could truly ever want me anyway. But, whatever the reason, an affair was simply never an option.

I had only one friend who ever confessed to me that she had had an affair. I immediately stopped being her friend. I was aware of affairs going on in the movies and in soap operas – but I'm aware of a lot of things I see in the movies and on TV that are not a part of my life. In my mind, having an affair just isn't something any 'decent' person would do. To me having an affair was wrong – ultimate betrayal of a relationship – something that could only make you feel guilty – something to hide – something dirty.

My husband and I had had good times, and we had struggles. Our focus was our family – raising our children, going to church, doing the best we could. On the surface we were a perfect happy little family. There's no one thing in particular I can say was wrong in our marriage, but something wasn't right – so after 22 years of marriage, we decided to separate and get a divorce.

And now, here is my friend, Alan Sholar, telling me he wants us to 'get together.' It pissed me off. I had known Alan for about 15 years and thought he was one of the nice guys. Now, here he was asking me to do something I believed was so terribly wrong – he wanted us to get together.

Our families had met when we all attended the same church. His mom and my mom became best friends and Alan and his older brother, Ricky, ran around with my sister, Mitzi, back when they were in high school and as young adults. I'm four years older than my sister, so at the time she and the Sholar boys were friends running around together I had already been married for several years. I would only see Alan briefly when he would be at mom's to hang with Mitzi. Neat kid; always smiling;

good personality – but he was one of Mitzi's friends so I was never really around him very often.

Not long after my becoming acquainted with the Sholar family they moved into a house across the street from me and my husband. One snowy day in the winter of 1980, the neighborhood kids got together to go sledding in the Sholar's back yard. My son, who was four years old, wanted to go sledding with the rest of the kids, so we joined in. It was so much fun – my little boy laughing and having the time of his life as we rode the sled down the hill together.

I don't know what caused me to do so, but for some reason I decided to go down the hill on the sled alone. As I went speeding down the hill the sled stopped suddenly when it hit a patch of mud where the snow had been worn down . . . but I didn't stop. I was flung forward and as I flew off the sled, my left leg hit a rock and broke near the ankle.

What an embarrassing experience. Here I was, weighing around 250 pounds at the time, lying at the bottom of a snowy hill with a broken leg and incapable of getting back up the hill. Several of the kids went running to the Sholar's door to get help.

Mr. Sholar, Alan, and Ricky came down to evaluate the situation and try to figure out how they were going to get someone of my size, with a broken leg, back to the top of the hill. Finally, someone suggested I lay face down on the sled as the Sholar's, and the kids, surrounded me, some pulling, some pushing, and all struggling to get my big butt back up the hill. I felt so very humiliated. It didn't bother me that my leg was broken. What bothered me was the difficulty everyone was having struggling to get me to the top of the hill and into the car so I could be taken to the hospital.

It was Alan who volunteered to drive me to the hospital. He didn't just take me to the hospital and drop me off, but went in with me to help get me where I needed to be. An example of how nice this kid always was – at least that's how I saw him – as just a really nice kid. After all, he was six years younger than me and although I was only 25 years old, he was just 19, and a 19 year old is still a kid to a married woman who has a son.

Once we got to the hospital, the first thing they did was wheel me into the X-ray room. A nurse there was asking all sorts of questions, name, age, address, etc., etc., etc. "Are you her husband?" she asked Alan. This skinny little kid kinda shrugged his shoulders, smiled from ear to ear, turned crimson red, lowered his head and said, "Nawww..." as he shyly shook his head from side to side.

"My husband is at work," I volunteered the information. "I'm sure someone will call him and let him know I'm here. He works on a horse farm and it's not always easy to reach him. It might be a while before he can get here."

"OK, Mrs. Thompson," the nurse said, "you'll have to step up on this stool to get on the x-ray table and lie down so we can get some x-rays of your ankle. The x-ray tech will be here in a few minutes." She then left the room.

I pulled myself out of the wheelchair and looked down at the little metal step-stool she had referred to. It was at least six inches high. *"Yeah, right,"* I thought, *"here I am five foot three, nearly as wide as I am tall, have a broken ankle and I'm gonna 'step up' onto a stool to get on a table that is a height practically level with my boobs. How the hell am I supposed to do that?"*

I guess Alan could sense my concern over trying to figure out just how I was going to accomplish getting up on the x-ray table and said, "I'll sit you up there." I couldn't see that happening either. Alan was tall, nearly six foot, but I bet he didn't weigh 120 pounds soaking wet. I know I weighed more than twice his weight. I have no idea how that skinny kid did it, but he picked me up and sat me on the table.

"Thanks," I said, still somewhat shocked that I was now sitting on the cold hard x-ray table.

The x-rays were completed and after a while a nurse came in to tell me the bone just above my left ankle was indeed broken – like I didn't know that already. She also informed me it would be several hours before the orthopedic surgeon could arrive and take a look at the x-rays. During that time I would have to sit in one of the exam rooms and wait for his arrival. She wheeled me into the exam room, left me sitting in the wheel chair, put a pillow on top of a stool, propped my broken leg onto the pillow, then left the room – but Alan didn't leave. He stayed at the hospital with me keeping me company until my husband arrived. Once I had someone else around to look after me Alan left.

They operated on my leg the next day and put me in what they called a walking cast. I was off work only two weeks. The Sholar's didn't live across the street from us much longer after the broken leg incident, so I never really got the opportunity to thank his dad, brother, and especially Alan for everything they had done for me that day. At the same time, I was also embarrassed at the idea of seeing them face-to-face, remembering what a struggle it had been to get me back up that snowy hill and how humiliated I felt because of my size.

A couple months after my sledding accident the Sholar family moved into the county onto the Conlee farm. Mom would go there to play Rook with Alan's mom and dad. Occasionally she would ask me to drive her to the Sholar's when they needed a fourth player for the Rook game. I remember one occasion in particular when Alan happened to be there. I finally had the opportunity to have a one-on-one conversation with Alan where I was able to thank him for all he had done to help me out on that snowy day when I had broken my leg. Of course, the memory of the broken leg and being pushed and pulled back up the hill was not a fond one for me, but somehow Alan saying "no problem – I enjoyed helping" made me feel better about the whole situation.

I don't remember what else our conversation may have been about that day, but I do remember him smiling a lot, making me laugh, and how comfortable and happy I felt in his company. That brief encounter with Alan had caused his transformation in my mind – he was no longer a kid but had grown into a nice young man. I left the Sholar's house that night feeling . . . happy.

A couple weeks later I went with mom once again to the Sholar's but this time Alan wasn't there. The mood was totally different. Although the Rook game with mom and Alan's parents was fun and the atmosphere friendly, the feeling just wasn't the same. I felt disappointed because Alan wasn't there. Right then I told myself, *"Bobbie, you can't come back here again."* I was sure it wasn't right for me to want to be in the company of this nice young man and it especially couldn't be right for me to be disappointed because he wasn't there – no matter how innocent the visit might be. Although mom continued to go to the Sholar's to play rook, I choose to never go back.

While living on the Conlee farm, Alan's mom gave birth to his little sister. Alan was 20 years old. Soon after his little sister was born, the Sholar's moved back to our neighborhood – only now they lived a block away instead of just across the street.

I gave birth to my daughter on August 18, 1982 – our 10th wedding anniversary – the greatest anniversary present any woman could ever receive – a beautiful baby girl. I remember Alan's mother bringing his little sister over to our house to see 'da baby' – that's what his little sister kept saying as she walked into the house, 'see da baby.' She, herself, was just a baby – only one year old – but I thought it was so precious how eager she was to see 'da baby.'

Although Alan and I were rarely in one another's company, we somehow were made aware of what was going on in one another's lives through our family's friendships. Alan continued to run around with my sister until he married. The two girls, my daughter and his little sister, grew up as friends and played together often, attending one another's birthday parties upon occasion, and the same schools. Our moms continued to remain best friends and visited one another often.

Even though we never really had much direct connection, we live in a small town, so upon occasion I'd see him with his wife, and as time passed, with his wife and son, at the local grocery store or we'd pass in the streets just long enough to say "hello, how 'ya doing."

But no matter where I would see him, he always had a warm friendly air about him and was always smiling – always making me glad when I got the opportunity to say hello.

It was mainly through our mom's friendship that we were always semi-aware of what was going on in one another's lives. Mom would tell me something about Alan that his mom had said, or his mom would tell him something about me that my mom had said. That's how he had come to know that my husband and I had separated and were getting a divorce – my mom told his mom and his mom told him.

Now, here is a friend, who I've known at least 15 years, who I'd watch grow from a kid into a man, who I'd seen many times with his wife and son, telling me he wants us to 'get together.' I couldn't believe this nice man had turned into one of those guys. When guys said something like this to me previously all I could do was be insulted, turn my head, and walk away. This time, though, my friend was saying it. This time I could do something about it. I knew Mary, his wife – I could tell on him. I could get his goose cooked.

"Well, Mr. Married Man," I huffily hissed, "When your wife says you can come fuck me that's when you can come fuck me." I was so pissed off.

Without hesitation he said, "She's here, I talked to her about it before I called you, she says it's OK, do you want to talk to her?"

I thought, *"I bet he talked to her about wanting us to get together. He could put any woman on the phone and have them say she's Mary. I'm not talking to someone on the phone; I'm going to their house and talk to Mary face to face. He'll be sorry for telling me he wants us to get together."* "No," I replied, "I'm coming to your house and talking to her in person."

That's exactly what I decided to do – go talk with Mary in person. I'd show him – I'd burn him. How dare him call me and act like a low life telling me he wants us to get together. Who the hell does he think he is? I'll show him. I'll tell Mary about his little phone call and she'll take care of him. By the time I get finished talking with Mary I bet he'll think twice before he approaches another woman about getting together.

I'm sure steam was rising from my ears as I drove the few miles over to Alan's house. I entered the front door of the split foyer house, probably without even knocking, and Alan was standing at the top of the stairs. "Is she here?" I asked rather sarcastically.

"I'm here," Mary answered from behind him, "Alan said you might be on your way over to talk to me."

As I walked up the stairs I said, "I bet he didn't tell you what I want to talk to you about, did he?"

"Sure he did," she said.

I thought, "*I just bet he did – wonder what he really told her.*" I said, "Really? What did he say it was about?"

She pointed to the chairs at the kitchen table and we all sat down as she continued, "He told me it's because he wants to have a physical relationship with you. He wants to have sex with you."

For the second time within the last hour I was stunned. "And this is OK with you?" I asked in a tone that showed my surprise, disbelief, and lack of understanding.

"We live an open-relationship lifestyle," Alan started to explain, "We've agreed we'd never do anything behind one another's back so when either one of us has any type of desire or urge we discuss it with one another before we move on our desires."

"I was asking your wife, I want to hear what SHE has to say about it," I said as I looked at Alan disapprovingly. I still wasn't too sure exactly what was going on here.

Mary sat directly across the kitchen table from me and looked me dead in the eye as she started speaking, "Bobbie, Alan's telling you the truth. He and I have discussed the fact that he would like to experience a physical relationship with you – to have sex with you. Sex can be just an enjoyable physical act between two consenting adults you know."

No, I didn't know sex could be 'just an enjoyable physical act.' I thought sex was an act of love between a husband and wife – I couldn't imagine sex being 'just physical.' No one had ever told me sex could be just physical. I guess that's something I'd missed out on learning by getting married so very young. I'd been told in church that just physical sex was wrong – was sin.

"Damn!" was all I could say. "You have an open marriage. You just have sex with someone else whenever you want?"

"That's kinda right, but not exactly the way it is. Bobbie, I love my husband, and it's because I love him that I'm open to sex outside the marriage. I'd much rather be open to discussing each other's desires and deciding together what steps to take in regard to acting upon those desires than for either one of us to be like lots of other people who are out there running around without their spouse knowing. We see 'cheating' as when the spouse is unaware. The way we see it, what makes it cheating is the dishonesty. And we don't just go around having sex with everybody."

My HUSBAND Looks Better in Lingerie Than I Do ... DAMN IT

"So, you guys are what they call swingers? I've heard about swingers but have never met anyone who is a swinger."

"Maybe you haven't, but maybe you have. An open relationship, or swingers, isn't something folks just go around broadcasting, but it's quite common," Alan said joining the discussion once again. "There are swinger magazines, swinger clubs, and swinger parties – there couldn't be all these things without enough swingers out there to support them. Who's going to publish a magazine devoted to swingers if there are no swingers to buy it? Having an open marriage is a way of life for lots of couples."

Then Mary said, "Look, we both know you and have known you for a long time, Alan even longer than me. There's no reason for me to be jealous because we believe a swinger situation is something that is strictly physical – in a swinger situation there's no room for the emotional connection that causes jealously. I know you're not trying to take my husband. I know you're clean, disease free, and drug free. I'd know where he is and that he's safe when he's with you. I know it's simply a physical relationship desired by my husband.

I've given lots of thought as to whether or not to give my permission for Alan to have a sexual relationship with you. I know if I told him I didn't want him to, then he wouldn't. It's because it IS you that I am receptive to the idea. If he had wanted to have sex with someone of lesser quality of character or someone I didn't know as well as I know you, then I may have said no. But, because it's YOU, then he has my permission. Whether or not it happens is now up to you."

"Well," is all I could say because that was the only response I could come up with at that moment. I don't know if it was the words she said, the tone she used as she said them, how comfortable I felt hearing what she was saying, or exactly what it was, but, somehow she made sense to me – it sounded logical. Mary's explanation of cheating – something done without the spouse's knowledge – gave me a different perspective of what I'd always called an affair. I'd never considered it was possible for a married person to have sex WITH the spouse's knowledge – and even approval. This was a totally new concept for me.

I had this sense of feeling that their relationship was more solid because of their willingness to be open and communicate with one another. How many times had I wanted to say things to my ex-husband but failed to do so because I simply couldn't bring myself to broach the subject or topic? How many times had I wanted to say, "Let's try this" or "do it this way" but never had the nerve. "Communication," our marriage counselor/preacher had said to us, "is of vital importance in a marriage." I sensed a bond of love between Alan and Mary that I couldn't help but admire – I think it was their ability to communicate, to discuss anything and everything that made me admire what they had together.

I had made the short trip to Alan's house to get him into trouble – but it was me who got something – an introduction to a lifestyle I'd never been aware of before. Mary's explanation gave me a different perspective – the difference between an affair (cheating) and an open lifestyle. I'd been raised to believe it's of utmost importance to be true to your word. I had said, "When your wife says you can…then you can." I felt a strong conviction that I had to honor my word. I was single and I wouldn't be hurting anyone by having a sexual relationship with Alan. The only person who could have gotten hurt was giving me her permission. "OK," I said, "we'll see where this goes." We set the day and time for our date to get together and I left with all sorts of new thoughts running through my mind.

The day arrived for our date and to say I was nervous would be a grave understatement. Right on time my doorbell rang. I opened the door and could immediately tell he was nervous as well.

"Come in," I said and we walked to the couch and sat down. I don't remember exactly what all we talked about, but we talked, and we talked, and we talked for what seemed like forever. I'm sure we had lengthy discussions on the weather, politics, and probably even religion. Well, maybe we left religion out of this particular conversation. But what we did NOT talk about was sex.

Finally I said, "Well, if we're going to do this I guess we'd better go into the bedroom. Although, I'm not really sure I'm able to do this. I've been married for 22 years and my self-esteem, especially when it comes to my body size, is so bad I didn't even want my husband to see me naked. Now, I'm supposed to get naked in front of you?"

"You're a beautiful sexy woman," Alan said, "and it has nothing to do with your body but what comes from inside you – your spirit, your personality."

Somehow those words enabled me to become calm enough to walk down the hallway and into the bedroom. I went around to one side of the bed and him the other.

We just stood there for a moment facing one another, not really knowing what to do next. After all, we had been friends for a long time and a lot was at stake here – our families were friends – if this got out, how would their friendships be affected.

"OK," he said, "we'll get undressed at the same time then get under the cover. Maybe that will help us get more comfortable."

We turned our backs to one another and undressed. As we faced each other my eyes immediately went low, and his high – "WOW" – was all either one of us could say – and we said it simultaneously. We had both seen a naked body before, but neither of us had seen body parts that . . . BIG.

He climbed under the covers from his side of the bed, and I climbed under the covers from my side of the bed and we met in the middle, yet, I was still not quite sure of what to do next, so Alan reached over and kissed me. He kissed me once more then I felt his warm hand on my breast. It only made me more nervous. "Stop," I said loudly. "I have to tell you something before we decide whether or not to go any further."

He looked at me as if he couldn't believe I had just told him to stop, but stop he did. Then I began, "I'm sure it's because I'm so fat, but I've never had much self-esteem when it comes to my sexuality. I know it is all because of how I see myself, but I think I'm repulsive. I'm so fat I wouldn't want to be with me and I can't imagine anyone ever being attracted to me. I couldn't even imagine my husband wanting me. I know it's all because of how I see myself, but the fact is that's how I see myself. Such a lousy self-image makes for a lousy sex life, so, if nothing happens here today, I want you to know it's not you, it's me.

Then Alan spoke, "Bobbie, you are a beautiful sexual being. You simply haven't been using your sexual pleasures, so you've stored them away safely in a treasure chest in the attic of your mind. We're going to open that treasure chest and take out one sexual pleasure at a time, unwrap it, then learn how to use that pleasure to your satisfaction. As you become comfortable with that pleasure it will begin to shine. Once it shines we're going to set it up high within your mind never to be hidden away again – to shine brightly. Then we'll remove the next sexual pleasure from the chest where you've safely stored it for so many years. We'll do the same with it – unwrap it – explore it until it is all aglow – then set it up for it to shine brightly never to be hidden away again. Then we'll remove another then another again and again, introducing you to each one until your mind is all aglow and you are able to gain satisfaction from each of your sexual pleasures without hesitation."

"Damn, that was good" I thought, *"take me, take me now,"* but I could never have said it.

"Now," he said, "let me look at you."

And I did.

* * * * * * * * *

When my ex-husband moved out my son had gone to live with his father and my daughter would go to be with them every other weekend. When she was gone is when Alan and I were able to get together. Our relationship had been going on for a couple months and I was enjoying a truly satisfying sex life – it was working perfectly for me. I could at least see how to get around in the attic of my mind – it was no longer dark, but not yet brightly lit either. Alan had such a way of planting seeds and watching them grow. He'd first make subtle comments about a subject or an idea, like oral sex for example, and then bring the subject more and more into the conversation until the idea would grow full bloom and we would have unwrapped yet another sexual pleasure and made it fully glow. I could not believe what was going on within me. I believed I was sexy – short fat me – sexy.

One day he dropped a seed that caused me to pause – the idea of a threesome. I believed most men desire to have a threesome – at least that's what the movies lead us to believe. But how many men have the nerve to actually approach their wife with the idea – probably not many, so it forever remains just a dream, a fantasy. But I didn't see Alan as being like most men. He was aggressive. He went for what he wanted. After all, he came after me hadn't he – and that took guts.

One evening I was lost in the pleasure of having sex with this aggressive man when he said, "I'd like to have a threesome with you and Mary. I can just imagine having the two of you at the same time – that would be a dream come true for me."

His words shocked me. Everything came to a sudden stop. "Well, that's never gonna happen," I quickly snapped, "There's not a lesbian bone in my body. There's no way I'm ever having sex with a woman."

"I'm not asking you to have sex with a woman. I'm asking you to have sex with me while I'm having sex with two women. The two of you would never have to touch one another – unless you choose to. You know it wouldn't be any big deal if the two of you did decide to get together; after all, a body is a body is a body. But, that would be up to the two of you. I'd never expect you to do anything you don't want to do. I'd just like to see what it would be like to have sex with you two women at the same time – I've always wondered if I am man enough to handle two women. Now, where were we?" he said then leaned forward and kissed me. It didn't take long for me to once again loose myself in the pleasure of the moment.

"A body is a body is a body" were the words he'd said. For some reason, those words stuck in my mind. How could that be true? I was very much aware of the differences between a man's body and a woman's body – and they are NOT the same. They taught us the differences way back in middle school. I couldn't understand, "a body is a body is a body" but I couldn't get the words out of my head either.

"I'm not asking you to have sex with a woman, but to have sex with me while I have sex with two women" were also words he had spoken that I couldn't get out of my head. Putting it that way was a totally different perspective from anything I had imagined. He's a patient man and continued to cultivate the threesome seed he had planted by occasionally commenting on how he imagined it would be for him if he could "pleasure two women at the same time."

I listened to his words and he always made it clear that it was his desire for HIM to have sex with two women – he never made it about ME having sex with anyone other than HIM. He had done so very much for me, how could I possibly say no to having sex with him, something I was doing already anyway – the only difference was, someone else would be in the bed with us. Apparently the lights from the sexual pleasures in my mind had begun to shine more brightly than I realized because I finally consented.

I arrived at their house at the appointed time and was greeted at the front door with a glass of wine – for which I was very thankful. The TV was on and porn was playing. I liked the heightened sexual energy and the eroticism, but when I saw the women in the movie there went my body image thing – my body simply NEVER looked like any of the beautiful, fit, young women in those movies – and now I was going to let someone else see my body – an experience I'd only shared with a select few. I quickly guzzled that first glass of wine then asked, "May I have more wine please?"

After a couple more glasses of wine, Alan led us to the bedroom. As we all undressed my attention went to Mary's body. We were both about the same height and both brunette, but she was smaller than me in size. She took off her top and I noticed how her breasts were much smaller than mine. She was a little pudgy in her mid-section, and her legs were thin. This was the first time in my life I had the experience of seeing another 'real live woman' naked. I almost immediately felt better about myself – because for the first time in my life I truly realized 'REAL WOMEN DON'T LOOK LIKE THE ONES IN THE MAGAZINES, ON TV, and IN THE PORN MOVIES.'

I saw ME totally differently – Yes, I was overweight, but my shape was in proportion from top to bottom – large, full, firm breasts; a definite waist that is a few inches smaller than my bust size; large round hips; and strong legs to hold it all up – I FELT SEXY – I was large, full, round . . . and desirable. Alan had made me believe he desired me, but I could never understand why he desired me. That day I finally got it – I finally understood – I am sexy and I am desirable. It took me personally seeing another real woman naked to realize the truth about myself. I left that day feeling desirable and sexier than I could have ever imagined. I was beginning to learn to accept and appreciate me just the way I am.

As the months passed Alan and I continued both our friendship and sexual relationship – friends in public and around our families – lovers when the opportunity presented itself. One incident with Alan that has always burned bright in my memory is a time when he told me about a dream he had. He said, "In my dream I had just arrived home from work and walked over to the kitchen table to put my lunch box down. 'Honey, I'm home,' I said and heard a reply come from down the hall, 'I'm in here. I'll be there in a minute.' As I let go of the lunch box and turned around my 'wife' emerged from one of the bedroom doors. She came down the hall toward me and gave me a welcome home kiss. Only, it wasn't Mary, it was you."

"That dream can never come true; I'm not a home wrecker." I said. "And like Mary said in our first conversation together when we started this relationship, I didn't set out to take her husband, only enjoy him."

Ours was a good relationship. He was my friend and lover and I thoroughly enjoyed his company no matter which role he was playing. He helped me when things needed to be repaired around the house, and the sex was completely satisfying. Although we enjoyed our friendship and lovers relationship, the lovers part had to be kept quiet. After all, our families were closely entwined and we didn't want to do anything to jeopardize those friendships.

Alan continued introducing me to the sexual treasures I'd stored away in my mind by bringing up new possibilities. He was always gentle when he'd bring up something else for us to try – like he had been with planting the seeds of having a threesome. The next seed he planted was that of multiple partner sex – to add a man to the threesome. I'd come so far in losing any inhibitions that it was much easier for me to accept the idea of adding another man to the mix than it had been to accepting the idea of a threesome.

He made the arrangements and the four of us got together at Alan and Mary's house. When I arrived it was the same setting as before – several glasses of wine and porn playing – only this time instead of heading to the bedroom there were blankets on the floor and the porn continued to play. It didn't take long for the wine to wash away any remaining inhibitions I might have had and everyone become lost in the pleasure of enjoying one another.

Soon after having the multiple partner experience I told Alan I was more comfortable when it was just one-on-one with us together and I wanted to go back to that. "If not for you, I would never have had such experiences. I can't imagine doing anything like that with anyone other than you. Sometimes I still can't believe you were able to get me to overcome my inhibitions to such a degree. I just know I couldn't have done it without you."

"Like I said in the beginning, those treasures have always been stored in the attic of your mind. They're in most people's minds – but most people simply won't do what it takes to enjoy them. I'm just glad I'm the one to help you unwrap yours."

Although our sexual relationship continued, over time we saw one another less frequently, but we did continue to get together whenever we had an opportunity. It was just that the opportunities didn't come that often. My life started getting busy and too many things demanded my attention. I had started running around with a couple of my girlfriends. We liked going out, but the only time I would go is when my daughter would be with her dad, which was every other weekend. I couldn't go out with them and be with Alan at the same time, which meant Alan and I saw one another less often.

I had also started dating and soon realized I was comparing every man I met with Alan. I believe it was Alan's take charge masculine aggressiveness coupled with his gentleness that had caused me to perceive him as the ideal man. Although I was dating, I never sought a commitment with anyone. A committed relationship represented pain to me. I simply didn't want to get into another relationship, and especially not a marriage, because it hurt so much when my marriage had ended in divorce. Divorce was the hardest experience I'd ever had in my life – just because it was the right thing to do doesn't mean it was an easy thing to do.

Getting divorced, raising my daughter alone, and being responsible for taking care of everything caused me to become a stronger person. All the decisions were mine alone to make and I had learned to make them quickly. I didn't have the luxury of taking the time to be wishy washy. Things had to be handled, and I had to handle them. I was becoming a bold, aggressive, independent woman. My friends would tease, "You'll be single the rest of your life because you've grown balls bigger than most men." I figured that was their way of saying I have control over my life, but I figured, if I didn't control my life, then who would? And, I agreed, it would take a bold man with bigger balls than mine to get my attention. After all, I didn't want to be saddled with a wimp. If any man were going to share my life, they'd have to be all man – a take charge, aggressive sort of man – like Alan.

As a matter of fact, I always told any guy I dated, "when you're with me, you're with me, but when you're not, you're not. I'll never ask you where you've been or what you've been doing and what I do is none of your business. If you're looking for a wife you're talking to the wrong girl. But if you want someone to go out to dinner with or get together occasionally, then let's talk." I didn't date a great number of men, but the few I did date seemed to be OK with the situation. I remember the reply of one guy who said, "I don't want to date you – you sound like a man." He meant it as a put-down, but I saw it as one of the best complements I'd ever received. To me his reaction to my demands meant I truly was in charge of my life and I had the freedom to live it as I please.

Alan and I had been enjoying our lovers relationship for approximately three years when in early 1997 I met and started dating a man I referred to as 'little redneck.' We had been dating only a month or so before I realized I was changing my tune. I fought hard not to fall for this little redneck, but I knew I was in a losing battle with myself – a relationship was developing between us.

I, of course, very much appreciated Mary for sharing Alan with me, however, I was a single woman, so from my perspective, that made my side of our relationship different. I didn't need anyone's permission – except Mary's – to have a relationship with Alan. Once I realized I was beginning to have feelings for this little redneck, I knew the sexual relationship Alan and I shared had to end. I couldn't imagine me having an open relationship with someone I was committed to nor could I bring myself to cheat by having an affair behind his back. That just wasn't me.

I called Alan and asked him if he had time to come to the house. As always, his answer was, "Sure, I'll be right over." When he arrived I instructed him to take a seat on the couch. When he did I climbed onto his lap facing him so I could talk to him eye to eye. "You know the little redneck I've been dating – well, I think I'm beginning to have feelings for him. You know me and know I cannot continue our sexual relationship while building a relationship with him. We both knew we couldn't go on like this forever, and I believe we've come to our end."

"I had a feeling you were going to say something like that. Bobbie, don't end what we have – marry me." The words just blurted out of his mouth.

"Phhh, I can't marry you, you're already married, and like I've told you before, I'm not a home wrecker." Although my words were true, that was only part of the reason I could never imagine being married to Alan. Alan was accustomed to living an open-relationship lifestyle. I couldn't imagine ever living such a lifestyle with my spouse. I also wondered, if he were forced to give up the openness, would he privately continue the lifestyle – would he become a cheater. Neither option – open nor cheater – set very well with me, which made being married to Alan an impossibility in my mind.

"I know you're not a home wrecker and I don't know why I said that. I can't imagine ever leaving Mary," he said immediately.

"I can't imagine you ever leaving Mary either. The two of you are so much stronger in your relationship than most couples I know."

"So, we're done, we're finished?" he asked.

"We have come to the end of the sexual part of our relationship, but I hope we can remain friends. We were friends a long time before we became lovers."

"I hope so too. Well, I guess that means I should go."

"I've made no commitments to this little redneck as of yet," I said looking up at Alan with a smile on my face. "We do have right now to be together one last time – if you're interested."

Even as we headed to the bedroom to spend our last time together I felt the pain of our relationship ending. Even before he was gone, I began missing him. Our last time together was so bitter sweet. We both hated to see the evening come to an end.

02

THAT LITLE REDNECK

In early 1997 on a Friday afternoon a co-worker came to me and said, "Bobbie, you're dating now, aren't you?"

"Yes," I responded. "Why?"

"My husband works with this guy who has been separated from his wife for about three months now. He caught her cheating on him with her first husband. We were wondering if we could introduce you to him."

"Sure. I don't mind meeting people. You know I'm not looking for a relationship, but making a new friend is always nice."

"Cool. My husband and I bowl every Friday night and we'll see him there tonight. Can you just happen to stop by so we can introduce the two of you?"

"Not tonight. My daughter is home this weekend, so I need to go on home after work."

"How about next Friday night? Can we let him know to expect you there next Friday night? That way, if you like him you can spend some time with him, but if you don't you're not obligated to a date."

"Sounds good to me."

The following Monday the receptionist informed me

I had a call on line 2. "This is Bobbie," I answered in my usual way.

"Hi Bobbie," a deep masculine voice came from the other end of the line. "You don't know me, but I'm hoping we can change that. We're supposed to meet next Friday at the bowling alley, but I've heard only nice things about you, and am anxious to meet you. I was wondering if we could meet this evening. Can I take you to dinner?"

My first thoughts were, *"well, he's a take-charge type man who is bold enough to call me, so that's impressive, and, it is a free meal."* so I said, "Sure, but it will have to be an early dinner. I have a fourteen year old daughter and I don't like to leave her at home alone much, so I can't stay out very long."

"That's fine," he said, "I have a daughter too, she's 11, but she lives with her mother. I only get to be with her every other weekend."

We made arrangements to meet at LaFiesta Grande Mexican restaurant right after I got off work. I pulled into the parking space and before I could get out of my car, the driver of the car behind me decided to take the space next to where I'd parked, only he decided to back in – which put the driver's side of his car at my driver's side.

He had his head down looking into his side mirror as he maneuvered his car into the parking space. He briefly looked up in my direction showing the bluest blue eyes I'd ever seen. *"Wow,"* I thought. *"I hope he's the man I'm supposed to be meeting – impressive eyes."*

Before I could get completely out of my car the man in the other car stepped up to me and said, "Are you Bobbie?"

"Cool," I thought, *"the eyes are my dinner date – his eyes alone make it worth it that I accepted his dinner invitation."* He was barely taller than me, was wearing black jeans, a black t-shirt, and a black baseball cap. He had a full short beard – black – which made his blue eyes shine brightly. "Yes, I'm Bobbie," I said.

"Here, I brought you something," he said as he pulled a long stemmed purple rose from behind his back – the kind wrapped in clear plastic that you can pick up at a gas station.

"Thank you," I said as I took the rose and thought, *"that was sweet."* I couldn't help it but my immediate thoughts were, *"what a cute sweet bold little redneck"* and *'little redneck'* immediately became his name.

We were seated in a booth opposite from one another and he removed the baseball cap to reveal his thinning hair. "I'm sorry for the way I'm dressed, but I just got off work too. I normally wear black because the factory where I work is so dirty. I figure the grease and grime doesn't show up as much on black clothes as it would on anything else."

"No problem," I said, "black suits you."

Talk came easily. He told me a little about himself. How he had recently separated from his wife and had pretty much given her everything. They had filed for divorce, but it wasn't yet final. Then he said, "I don't even have a car yet. She took our car. The car I'm driving belongs to my grandmother. It's old and rarely ever used, but I'm thankful to at least have something to drive until I can get another car."

"I know what you mean. My car is old too. My ex took our new Ford Explorer along with the payments.

Although I was left with an old car, at least I don't have car payments. Unfortunately, though, old cars have a way of wearing out and right now I need new brakes."

"I used to own my own mechanic shop, that is until my tools got robbed a second time and I couldn't afford to replace them. I had insurance, but not enough to cover the cost of all the tools I lost. I'd be working on something and need a new tool and just go out and buy it – after a couple years of doing that I had practically anything I could ever need – I just never got around to increasing my insurance. After I got hit the second time I decided to just close up shop and go to work at the factory. I'll be glad to fix your brakes for you though."

"Well, thank you," I said but I thought, *"you've known me for what, 30 minutes and you're offering to fix my brakes – I doubt it."*

The next afternoon around 3:45 the receptionist called me and said, "Bobbie, your mechanic is at the front desk, he needs your car keys."

"My WHAT?" I said surprised at what I'd heard. She repeated, "Your mechanic is at the front desk and needs your car keys, can you bring them down?"

"Sure, I'll be right there."

I rounded the corner to enter the lobby and there standing in front of the receptionist desk was the little redneck, all dressed in black, blue eyes shining, grinning broadly. "I ran out during lunch to get the brakes for your car so I could get here as quickly as possible after I got off work. I get off at 3:30 and I know you get off at 4:30, so I figured now would be a good time to change your brakes. Where is your car?"

"It's in the parking garage."

"I'll have to pull it into a level spot, but I can easily change the brakes right here. Just take me to the car."

I took him to my car then returned to my office, but didn't get any more work done the remainder of the day. I was too flabbergasted and impressed that 'my mechanic' had shown up to fix my brakes. After work I returned to my car as he was taking it down from the jack, "All done," he said.

"How much do I owe you?" I asked.

"Nothing."

"Let me pay you something."

"Nope. I didn't do it for money; I did it because I like you."

"OK, then, let me at least buy you a drink or something." He agreed to let me buy him a drink and we went back to the restaurant where we'd met the evening before.

Again, I couldn't stay very long because my daughter was at home so when we left the restaurant he walked behind me as we were going to our cars. He said, "Ya know, I always did like them big bottom girls." At first I felt I should be offended that he had made a comment on the size of my bottom, but then I remembered that Alan had taught me some guys like girls like me and that I am desirable – even if I do have a big bottom – so I just took it as a complement and thanked him.

We continued meeting after work almost daily to share a drink and some time together. It turned out that the weekends my daughter was with her father; his daughter was with her mother, which gave us time to be together. After seeing him for a while I decided to take him up on his invitation to spend the weekend with him at his apartment. One Friday after work I followed him to the apartment. He made supper, we watched a movie then I spent the night – once again he impressed me.

The next morning he had gone down to retrieve something from his car when his phone rang. For whatever reason, I decided to answer the phone. "Hello," I said.

"I want to speak to my husband," the voice on the other end of the line said.

"He's stepped out for a minute –can you call back in about five minutes?"

"Who is this?" she asked, "the bitch that's been screwing my husband."

"No, I'm the bitch that's screwing your ex-husband – no, wait, that's not me, that's you – aren't you screwing your ex-husband? Isn't your ex-husband supposed to be moving in with you this weekend?"

Then she did something that surprised me. She softened her voice and said, "I made a mistake. I want my husband back. I want my family back together. But I can't get him back as long as you're in the picture."

"Then I'll step away." I said. "I never want it to be said that I ever came between a man and his family – I'm not a home wrecker. If you really want him back then I'll give you the opportunity to work things out. We haven't known one another that long anyway, so it's no skin off my nose to just bow out. But mark my words – if I hear that your ex has moved into your house – I'll be the first person knocking on this apartment door." With that I hung up the phone.

I was putting my things I'd brought with me to spend the night into my bag when Little Redneck came back into the apartment. "Where are you going?" he asked. "I thought we were spending the weekend together. I've made plans for the whole weekend."

I told him about the phone call and that I was giving him the chance to go back to his family. "She doesn't want me," he said, "She just doesn't want anyone else to have me. Like I told you, her first husband is moving in with her – into my house. She's just trying to come between you and me."

"That may be true," I said, "but it also may be true that she really does want her family back. I'll not stand in the way of a family getting back together. If she's not really interested in restoring her family we'll know soon enough. If her ex really does move in with her, then you can call me – but not before." Then I left.

About a week later I was at work and my co-worker said, "have you heard, Little Redneck's wife moved her ex-husband into their house yesterday." The next day I got a phone call, "You said we'd know soon enough whether or not she really wanted her family back together or if she just wanted to come between us – now we know – she just wanted to come between us." We immediately started seeing one another again.

We continued seeing one another nearly every evening after work and spending every other weekend together. He took me to meet his grandmother – his father's mother – Granny. He told me Granny had raised him. He told me he was the oldest of four children and his father had left his mother when he was only six years old. Even that young, he saw himself in the role of caregiver to the younger children – always trying to help his mother out in any way he could. When he was 10 years old he came home from school one day to find his belongings in grocery sacks sitting on the front porch. When he asked why, his mother said, "Because you have to go live with Granny." He didn't understand why his mother was making him go away. When he asked why, her reply was, "because you look so much like your father I can't stand the sight of you." He said that statement had caused a hurt within him that he still carried.

I rationalized what I thought might have happened and said, "Surely now that you're grown you understand how difficult it must have been for your mother trying to raise four small children. The best thing your mom could have ever done for you was to send you to Granny's to live. I'm sure it had to be hard on her to have to give you up. Maybe she said it that way so you wouldn't see how much she was hurting from having to send you away."

"May be . . . but that's not how I see it. I believe she loved the other kids, but she didn't love me."

As we spent time together he told me more and more about his life. He told me about his time spent in military service but explained that he had it easy because he was the mechanic for some highly ranked individual. He told me about the woman he had lived with while he was in the military – how good she was to him – and how he should have married her. He told me about being grandfathered in at his father's trucking company and driving an 18-wheeler through New York during a time the garbage collectors were on strike – how the city stunk from all the garbage lining the streets. He told me how he settled down and opened his mechanics shop after getting married and having a daughter.

He also told me he was a recovering alcoholic and a frequent visitor to Alcoholics Anonymous meetings. "I don't understand," I said. "How can you be a recovering alcoholic yet have a drink with me after work nearly every day. I don't have any experience with alcoholism, but I thought recovering alcoholics can't stop once they take a drink. I thought recovering alcoholics don't go to bars."

"I've learned to be in control over the alcohol," he said. "I know my limit – I've promised myself I'd get up and leave the bar once I've had a second drink to stop from taking the third, or fourth."

I admired his ability to be in control. I'd seen him do it. I'd been there when he'd have a drink or two, then we'd leave the bar. I just always thought he was leaving because I had to go – I hadn't realized he was leaving to keep himself from drinking.

I had lunch one day with my friend, Burlita, and was telling her about Little Redneck. I told her the things he had told me and that he had said he was a recovering alcoholic. "Bobbie," she said, "my father is an alcoholic and my brother is an alcoholic. I know what it's like to be around an alcoholic. If he's really an alcoholic my advice to you is to RUN, RUN AWAY, RUN AWAY FAST, RUN AWAY FAR."

On a Saturday morning a week or so after lunch with my friend I got a phone call from Little Redneck. "Can you come pick me up from jail and take me to my apartment?"

"Do WHAT? Jail, why are you in jail?"

"I got a phone call late last night from one of my neighbors. They told me there was a loud party going on at my house and my daughter was there. They told me I needed to come see about my daughter to make sure she was safe. I went to the house and sure enough the front door was open, loud music playing, and people I didn't know going in and out of my house. I got out of my car but before I went into the house I picked up a large wrench I had lying in the back seat. I didn't know what to expect when I got inside and I wanted to be prepared. I wanted to get my daughter. Once inside I was told my daughter wasn't there – she'd gone to spend the night with my sister – but because I had shown up, a fight started. I got arrested. Can you just come get me and take me home?"

"Sure," I said, "I'm on my way." It took me about half an hour to get to the jail and all the while I was thinking about the advice Burlita had given me – RUN AWAY. "That's it," I told myself, "I've had enough. He comes from an abusive childhood; he's a recovering alcoholic, fighting, getting arrested, and jail – way too much drama for me. It's over. I'm taking him to his apartment – I'm telling him I won't have this crap in my life, and then I'm leaving."

We arrived at his apartment and he immediately began scurrying around throwing his belongs into a clothes basket. "What are you doing?" I asked.

"I've got to get out of here. I've got two weeks before my court date and I have to stay out of trouble or I'm going to wind up spending time in jail. They told me at the party the other night when the police were taking me out that this wasn't over. They said they'd get me."

"What the hell did you do the other night anyway?"

"I told you, I went looking for my daughter. You

would have done the same thing if you thought your daughter was in danger."

He was right. I wouldn't care what I'd have to go through as long as my child was safe.

"Apparently someone saw me walk in with the wrench in my hand and called the police as soon as I got there. Once I learned my daughter wasn't there I turned around and started to leave – that's when the police showed up. One of the policemen told me I'd have to leave the premises and I said, "The premises just happens to be the house I own." Then he reached out to take the wrench but I held it up and away and said, "Hell no, I'll carry it out just like I carried it in." While I was holding it up someone from behind grabbed it, but I held onto it – there was a scuffle, and I was carried out and put into the police cruiser. I spent the night in jail, now here we are." He continued scurrying around tossing things into the clothes basket the entire time he talked.

"Who said this isn't over? Who threatened you?"

"I'm not really sure. I guess it was her first husband. I just know my temper and know if anyone tries to take me on they'll have a battle on their hands. I can't let that happen. I have to stay out of trouble. I can't go to jail. I can't take a chance on losing my job. I just need to get out of here for at least two weeks. My court date is in two weeks – if I can just stay away that long everything will calm down by then and everything will be OK."

"Where are you going? To Granny's?"

"No, that's too close. I have to get out of town. I'm not sure where I'll go, I'm just sure I can't stay here."

Then I heard this voice that at first I didn't recognize – it said, "Come stay with me." I even looked around to see if by chance there was someone standing behind me who had said those words. It actually took me a couple seconds to realize that the words had come from my own mouth.

"That'll work," he said, "I'm ready, let's go. I'll follow you."

We got to my house and as he was getting his things out of his car I went inside. My daughter was sitting on the couch doing homework. It wasn't until I stepped into the house that I felt the consequences of the words I'd spoken. Not once had I taken her into consideration regarding my actions. What had I done? What was I going to say? Why hadn't I thought of her first? *"Oh crap, I think I just became the worst mother in the world."*

"Little Redneck is going to be living with us for a while," once again, the words just shot out of my mouth without me even thinking.

"Do WHAT? When?" was my daughter's reply.

"Right now, he's getting his things out of the car now."

"MMMMmmoooooooooommmmm!!!!"

"That's just the way it is and you just have to deal with it." Then I thought, *"OK, with what I just said now it's official. I no longer think I'm the worst mother in the world -- those words just confirmed it."*

She slammed her books together, stomped into her room, and slammed the door. I felt horrible.

I didn't have to live with Little Redneck long before I realized he was always angry. He'd fuss about something or someone at work. He'd argue with his ex-wife. He'd get upset with the check-out clerk at the store and give them a hard time. Every other weekend when he'd pick up his daughter they would invariably spend their first hour together screaming at one another. Then, all of a sudden, his mood would change and the arguing would stop.

We'd been living together about a year when we got a heavy snow fall. We'd spent just one day in the house unable to get out and go anywhere or do anything and were already starting to go stir crazy. Early afternoon of the second day of being stuck inside we decided to chance the roads and go to Hancock Movie Warehouse and rent a couple movies to keep us from going insane. Little Redneck went out to the car to get it warmed up and clear away the snow. He'd been outside for about 15 or 20 minutes and I decided he'd had plenty of time to do what he needed to do, so I put on my coat and headed outside. As soon as I stepped out the door, he threw a snow ball at me. We immediately started playing in the snow, throwing snow balls, dodging snow balls, laughing like a couple of kids. All of a sudden he came running toward me, threw both arms around me, and tackled me as if he was a defensive football player and I had the ball. We both fell into the soft snow laughing. We'd barely stepped outside and our spirits were already lifted.

We made our way to the Movie Warehouse and selected our movies. We walked up to the counter to pay for the movies and I reached into my coat pocket for my wallet. "Oops," I said, "I must have forgotten to pick up my wallet. Guess you'll have to pay for the movies."

A frown came across his brow as he gave me an angry look. Then his look softened and he said, "No problem." He paid for our movie choices and we headed for the car. As soon as we got in the car he angrily said, "Where did you leave your purse, at some man's house?"

"Do what?" I said shocked at his tone and his question.

"You heard me. Who are you fucking behind my back?"

"I've simply left my wallet at home. How did you get from me forgetting my wallet to me cheating on you?"

We got back to the house and both began looking high and low for my wallet. We couldn't find it anywhere. The more we looked, the more aggressively he accused me of being at some man's house and leaving my wallet there. "That's what SHE did," he said, "she left her purse at her ex-husband's house. She told me her purse had been stolen, but then it showed up at the house a few days later. That's when I found out she'd been at his house and had left her purse there. You women are all alike – you lie and cheat then deny it."

"I'm not your ex. I don't lie. I don't cheat. I'm not like that," I said, but he never heard my words. For three days he continued his ranting and raving, over and over, "who are you screwing behind my back." He'd yell it at me from across the room. He'd get right up in my face pointing his finger and say, "Who is he. Who is it you're fucking? I'll find out." It was horrible.

On the afternoon of the third day the snow was nearly all melted and you could see patches of grass coming through the thin covering of what was left of the snow. I saw something in the yard near the place where he had tackled me and thrown me to the ground – it was my wallet. "Look," I said as I pointed in the direction of my wallet, "What's that over there on the ground."

He went out to see what it was and picked it up, "It's your wallet," he said.

"Apparently it fell out of my coat pocket when you threw me to the ground that day just before we went to rent our movies. You've put me through hell for three days and you're the reason my wallet came up missing to begin with."

He went back inside the house and I followed as he went into our bedroom. "I'm so sorry," he said, "I didn't mean to put you through hell. I know you love me. I know you wouldn't cheat on me." Then he started crying. "I don't know why I treated you like that. It's just that those same old feelings came up from when I found out she had been cheating on me." He started hugging me as he cried, "You're the best thing that's ever happened to me and I love you." The more he talked the harder he cried. "Everyone I've ever loved has abandoned me – my dad, my mom, my ex-wife. I guess I just expect you to abandon me someday too. You're too good to me – how can someone as good as you love someone like me?" By this time he was slumped in the floor sobbing.

I again rationalized as I sat in the floor with him, put my arms around him, and held him close to me. "You've just had a hard life. Someday you'll learn just how much I love you and that I'll never abandon you. Someday you'll learn that I'm not your ex-wife – I'd never do the things you've told me she's done." I just knew that 'someday' he'd learn.

Things did get better – for nearly a year. Then one Friday afternoon we were invited to celebrate a friend's birthday with drinks at LaFiesta right after work. We hadn't been there since he'd moved in with me, so we accepted the invitation. There were several friends there and we were having a good time. After two drinks I told Little Redneck I was ready to go home. I remembered what he'd said about having control over his drinking, and I didn't want to stay longer and be the cause of him falling off the wagon.

"You go on," he said, "I'll be right behind you."

This wasn't like him. I immediately felt uneasy, but went on home anyway. An hour later he still wasn't home. Then two hours. Then three hours. It was nearly midnight before he finally showed up and was in a rage like I'd never witnessed in my life before. He burst into the house yelling, "She told me all about you." Then he came over to me and pushed me up against the wall, pinning me there with his left arm up against my chest and his right hand in my face, finger pointing, yelling, "I knew you were fucking someone else, and she told me all about it tonight."

I could tell he was drunk, but he was so much more than just drunk. It was as if he was possessed by an angry demon. I don't know how I managed to do so, but I got away from him and went down the hall to my daughter's room. She was in bed. I reached around and locked her bedroom door then pulled it closed so he wouldn't be able to enter her room. Then I went into our bedroom, and he followed. He immediately threw me down on the bed and sat straddle my chest. He reached over and grabbed the phone receiver from the night stand next to the bed and yelled, "Call him. Call him right now. I want to know who the son of a bitch is that you've been fucking."

I struggled trying to get out from under him and yelled, "I'm not cheating. There is no one for me to call. I don't know what you're talking about."

But it seemed that the more I struggled, the stronger, and more enraged he became. "You're lying. I know you're lying, she told me she saw you with him in the parking lot. You either tell me or I'll beat it out of you." The next thing I saw was the phone receiver in his hand coming toward my head, *"Oh God,"* I thought, *"he's going to beat me to death with the phone receiver and my daughter is in the other room. Please, God, help me."*

I moved my head just as the receiver hit the pillow. The force of the blow caused him to lose his balance and he fell onto the bed. It was as if God was telling me what to do as I thought, *"Don't fight. Don't struggle. Talk softly. Be calm."* Then I calmly and softly said, "Honey, you know I love you and I'd never cheat on you." He never responded, because he immediately passed out. I lay next to him exhausted from the experience, relieved that I had escaped death, and crying all night.

The next morning he didn't even remember anything that had happened the night before. I told him it didn't matter whether he remembered or not, I did and I wouldn't live like that. I kicked him out. Several times a day he'd call me saying he was sorry, he wanted to talk with me, he loved me, and vowed to never drink again. He sent flowers to me at work. He apologized over and over asking me to give him another chance. He sent more flowers. After several days I finally gave in and agreed to meet him for dinner after work – we chose to meet at a restaurant where alcohol was not served.

He again told me how much he loved me, that I was the best thing to ever enter his life and he didn't want to lose me. He vowed, "I promise I will never take another drink as long as I live if you will just let me come back." From my perspective I knew he had it in him to be a good person. Everyone who knew him liked him. He would give anyone the shirt off his back if he could help them. He was very charismatic, and I was the only person who ever saw the rage and anger.

"Ok," I said, "you can come back. But, if there is ever an instance I even smell any type of alcohol on your breath you're gone – no questions asked – no more chances given."

"As long as you'll have me, I promise I'll never take another drink." He moved back in the next day.

My daughter left home and moved into her first college dorm on August 18, 2000 – on her 18th birthday. I was devastated. I'd known for months exactly what day she'd be leaving, but I couldn't handle it. Her father had to come move her into her dorm because I didn't have the strength to get out of bed. I cried all day long. Somehow, though, the very next day when I woke up things seemed to be better. It was as if I had survived some sort of rite of passage by my child leaving our home to begin her own independent life. I told myself she hadn't left me, she had simply left home.

Little Redneck and I had been living together for nearly four years. There was something about my daughter leaving that seemed to make it OK for me to remarry, so, on November 4, 2000, Little Redneck and I were married. I cried all day long that day too.

Most of the time, I was happy. There was hardly a day go by that Little Redneck wasn't angry at this person or that person for some reason. But, as long as it wasn't me he was angry at, things were OK. However, about every four to six months he'd find something to be angry with me about and we'd have another big blow up – and it always lead to him accusing me of cheating. But somehow during the course of each blow up a different issue would be addressed and seem to get resolved and always end with him apologizing profusely, telling me how much I meant to him, telling me how much he loved me, and telling me he'd never hurt me again.

It was as if it had become my calling to pull him up out of the pits of despair and depression trying so very hard to get him to a point where he could stand on his own two feet. I just knew that ONCE HE LEARNED that I loved him and he was able to see our lives from my perspective, then he'd realize life is good and there would be no more need for all the rage and anger. If he could just learn.

I worked hard at keeping Little Redneck happy. It took all the strength I could muster struggling to pull him to his feet, and just about the time I began to believe he was able to stand alone, down he'd go again. The vicious cycle continued over and over again – we'd go through another big blow up – some issue would be resolved during the process – he'd apologize and promise never to do it again – I'd believe him and spend all my strength trying to get him to his feet again.

Each time I wanted so very badly to believe this really would be the last time he'd hurt me. I held on to my belief that he'd eventually learn that I loved him, I'd never cheat on him, he had nothing to be angry about, and our life together could be a good one. I've heard that love is blind, and when it came to Little Redneck, I was definitely wearing blinders. When I looked into those sparkling blue eyes of his I saw a diamond in the rough shining through a dark soul. I knew there was such great potential buried behind those blue eyes – somewhere – even if no one else in the world could see it. Each time he blew up at me I thought another layer of the darkness was being stripped away bringing that shining diamond closer to the surface for all the rest of the world to see.

We'd been married for only a year before the anger, accusations, and fits of rage accelerated in intensity and increased in frequency. It was like having a dog you enjoy petting, but never know when he'll attack and rip the juggler vein right from your neck. Then after biting and tearing you to pieces, leaving you wounded yet still alive, the dog would start wagging his tail and come over for you to pet him some more. At first you're reluctant to reach out to pet the dog, but he stands there, wagging his tail, licking your wounds, trying his best to get you to pet his head. Just about the time you began healing from the previous attack and get into enjoying petting the dog, believing he'd learned a lesson and would never attack again, you get caught off guard and the dog once again attacks. It's amazing what blind love – or maybe it was stupidity on my part – allowed me to endure.

Early one morning in mid-July of 2002, little redneck was getting ready for work. He was accustomed to working overtime, but his overtime was always to go in early in the morning about three or four hours before the shift started instead of staying later at the end of the day. He was in the dining room putting on his work boots when his cell phone rang – it was about 3:00 a.m. I woke up just a few minutes prior and had gotten out of bed to get a drink of water. I saw him look at the number on the phone, push the button to stop the ringing, then lay the phone back down on the table. About that time he saw me come into the room, so he picked the phone back up and turned it completely off.

"Who was that," I asked as he went back to putting on his boots and I filled my glass with water.

"Just a wrong number," he said.

I thought, *"I can't even imagine the hell I'd have to endure if I got a phone call at 3:00 in the morning that happened to be just a wrong number."*

He then went into the other room so I walked over and picked up the phone, turned it back on, then hit redial for the last incoming call. A woman immediately answered and said, "Hey baby, you still want that blow job this morning."

It was as if I had been punched in the face and I couldn't control the gasp that came from my mouth. "Hello, hello" she said on the other end of the phone.

It took me a second or two to regain my breath before I was able to say, "And just who do you plan on giving a blow job to?"

"Oh my god," I heard her say, "It's his wife." Then the line went dead.

That's how I learned he was having an affair. There was no amount of his rage or anger that hurt me as badly as learning my husband was a cheater. He continued to swear it was a wrong number and that he had no idea who was on the other end of the line. I so very badly wanted to give him the benefit of the doubt. After all, it was possible the phone call had been for someone else's husband. I had to know one way or another – either prove him guilty, or prove him innocent. We live in a small town, and it only took a couple weeks of asking around before I learned he was having an affair with a woman who worked at our local Kroger store, where he had taken on a part-time job.

Somehow, me learning that *HE* was cheating caused the accusations and fits of rage to come more frequently and more aggressively – to the point that there were a couple times I thought to myself, *"OK, so this is the way and this is the day I'm going to die."* However, even in the midst of the worst time of my life, I truly believed that if somehow he could understand – if he could just learn – that I loved him, then the cheating would stop and our life together could be good. I tried to salvage our marriage and talked him into going to marriage counseling. I feared the pain of going through a divorce again more than I feared a life of misery with a cheating husband.

Someone recommended Dr. Stith so we went to our first marriage counseling session together in mid-August. I poured my heart out to the counselor about what I had endured being with Little Redneck over the last six years. Then it was Little Redneck's turn to speak. I couldn't believe what he said. He told her I was going through the change of life and he never knew what kind of mood I might be in whenever he approached me. He said that living with me was like walking on egg shells. I couldn't believe the lies that came from his mouth. The time for our counseling session ended and Dr. Stith suggested we make separate appointments for our next session.

Right in the middle of all this drama and chaos, the day came that I had been looking forward to for years – my last day of work. I'd started working for Kentucky

State Government in 1973 right after I graduated from high school. I'd put in my time and retired effective September 1, 2002. I was only 47 years old and was proud that I had accomplished retiring at such a young age.

My daughter came to the house to pick me up and take me out to dinner to celebrate my retirement. As we drove to the restaurant she started questioning me about Little Redneck, "Mom, I don't understand, why do you let him treat you that way."

"Honey, he's just had a hard life. Eventually he'll learn . . ." but before I could finish my sentence she said, "Mom, the things you're waiting for him to learn, he should have learned a long time ago. If he hasn't learned by now, he's not going to. He'll never change. I can't stand to see you be treated so badly."

Her words stunned me. I thought, *"Oh my god, how did my beautiful baby girl become so much more intelligent than me at such a young age?"* I hadn't realized what she had seen and how it had affected her. I was acutely aware, once again, just how badly I had failed at being a good mother for her. I hated what I had put her through but was thankful she hadn't been around to see how the rage had accelerated since she'd moved out and we'd gotten married. How I wished I could turn back time and take Burlita's advice to run. If there were some way for me to do so, I'd gladly erase the last six years.

I attended my first alone session with Dr. Stith and she started by saying, "You know you're living in an abusive situation, don't you?"

"Bullshit," I thought, *"I'm an intelligent, in control, strong, independent woman. I would never allow anyone to abuse me."* I guess she could read the expression on

my face because she continued with, "You know not all abuse is physical. There is mental and emotional abuse as well. The rage and accusations you described to me in our first session are forms of mental and emotional abuse."

Then I spoke up, "You're wrong. I'm not living in an abusive situation. I'm smarter than that."

Even with all that had gone on over the last six years, I truly hadn't recognized what I had endured as 'abuse.' When I was in my early teens my mom had a friend who was a victim of abuse – I'd seen it happen. I knew what abuse looked like. We were at the friend's trailer one day and I was playing cards with her, my mom, and her friend's husband at the kitchen table. The husband was drinking the entire time we played. Then, for some reason, he just snapped. He pulled mom's friend from her chair by the hair of her head. She tried unsuccessfully to pull away. He would hit her – he punched her in the stomach, he punched her in the head, he punched her in the back. With each blow she struggled harder to get away from him.

Mom grabbed me to get me out of his way. We couldn't leave without going into the bedroom at the far end of the trailer to retrieve mom's purse with her car keys. As we came back down the hall to go out the door we passed the bath room, mom's friend was lying motionless in the bathroom floor. I thought she was dead.

The next day mom asked me to call her friend to check on her. I was so shocked when she answered the phone. I asked her if she was OK and she said, "Sure I'm OK, why?"

"The way your husband beat you last night I thought you were dead."

"Beat me? Honey, that was just a little spat. We fight like that all the time."

I couldn't believe it. I was surprised she was still alive, and she was acting as if it was no big deal. I vowed then and there no man would ever treat me that way.

Dr. Stith's voice pulled me out my memory of what abuse is to me by saying, "Really. When was the last time you told your sister about the things he's done to you?"

"I've never told my sister about what he's done."

"Why not?" she asked.

Without thinking I immediately said, "I don't want her to know how stupid I am for putting up with it." It was at that precise moment the blinders came down from my eyes. It was at that precise moment, hearing those unexpected words come from my own mouth, I realized I WAS living in an abusive situation. It was at that moment the love I had for Little Redneck died.

The entire time we had been together, whenever I looked at him all I saw was a bright blinding light – the diamond within. When I got home that day I looked at him and saw only the darkness. I tried hard to see at least some glimpse, some flicker of the light. I would turn my head first one way, then another, searching for the light – but it simply didn't exist. I was devastated. I had loved the light – and now it was gone.

Since I no longer had to go to work, my days at the house alone were peaceful and quiet – that is until Little Redneck got home. Then he would be screaming at me from the time he got home until time to go to sleep. "Who have you been fucking today? I don't believe you've just been sitting here all day by yourself. Did he come here or did you meet him somewhere?" Then he started missing work to stay home and babysit me. I had no way of escaping his torment. My nerves were shot. I was upset and felt sick all the time.

I told him he had to get out of my face and give me time and space if our marriage was ever going to be salvaged. I explained that in order for me to heal, I had to get away from him – he had to move out. He refused to leave. After two weeks of begging him to leave I said, "If you stay, my only alternative is to get a divorce and force you out." His reply was, "You'll never divorce me; I'll kill you first and no one will ever know I did it. I know how to fix your car so it will look like an accident and then I'll get your house and everything you own." And I believed him. Now, not only were my nerves shot, not only did I feel sick all the time, but now I was frightened too. The next time I was alone I called the police.

I don't know if it was him being aware that the police were now involved, but, for some reason he finally made the decision to move out. On September 30, 2002 he moved, but that's when the stalking began. He'd call me and say, "Did you see me watching you today? I saw you when you were driving down such and such road. I could have killed you then." I'd hang up and then he'd call back and say, "I'm sorry. It doesn't have to be this way. I love you. Please let me move back in."

I'd say, "I can't. I've not even yet begun to heal. You have to leave me alone. You have to give me time to heal."

Then he'd start screaming at me again, "I'll kill you yet you bitch," and I'd hang up, only for him to call and say again that he was sorry and that he didn't mean it.

My HUSBAND Looks Better in Lingerie Than I Do ... DAMN IT

I could never have dreamed my life would ever be so miserable.

He'd been out of the house and had stalked me for about three weeks when on Sunday, October 20, 2002 he called me and said in a very calm voice, "I just want you to know that I'm going to give you the time and space you need to heal because I love you and our marriage is important to me. I want you to know that I'll be here for you and if you need me for anything all you have to do is call and I'll come – but I'm not going to be contacting you – I'm giving you the time and space you've asked for."

I thought *"How wonderful – he's finally beginning to understood what it's going to take for me, and maybe even our marriage, to heal."*

On Tuesday evening they found his body in his apartment. The coroner determined that sometime Sunday afternoon – apparently right after hanging up the phone from his call to me – he picked up a gun, put it in his mouth ... and pulled the trigger. He was only 40 years old.

The day after his body was found a local newspaper had an obituary notice that read, '. . . a short illness resulted in the death of . . .' I thought, *"yep, when you put a gun in your mouth and pull the trigger you don't have much time to be ill."* I felt cheated that the truth hadn't been told. I thought a more truthful obituary would have read something like, "After cheating on and abusing his wife for years he apparently finely felt pangs of guilt and couldn't handle the feeling, so he shot himself."

That very day Alan called and said, "I saw an obituary with Little Redneck's name. That wasn't your husband was it?"

"Yes," I said and began to cry.

Alan continued, "I'm just calling to make sure you're alright. Let me know if there is anything I can do."

"Thanks," I said, "I appreciate the call, but there's nothing you can do," and we both hung up.

I tried to think back to recall just when the last time was that I had seen Alan. Then it dawned on me that during the previous six years it was rare that I had seen anyone who had been my friend before I got with Little Redneck. At that moment I realized I had been alienated from my friends without even being aware.

I was faced with the task of making the funeral and burial arrangements. When I met with the folks at the cemetery they asked if Little Redneck had been in the military. I told them he had, and they said he would be provided a marker for his grave indicating he was a veteran. They explained all they needed was a copy of his military discharge and that it could all be taken care of after the funeral.

The visitation and funeral services were pure hell. His family and co-workers treated me as if I had physically put the gun in his mouth and pulled the trigger. Woman after woman came to the visitation and flaunted the fact they had been with my husband. Apparently there had never been a time when he wasn't cheating on me and they chose his funeral visitation as the time and place to bring it to my attention. Granny, his daughter, and I were the only people who seemed to be there to grieve his loss.

A few days after the funeral I went to Granny's to get his military papers. His uncle was there and when I asked for the papers he said, "Honey, he was never in the military."

My HUSBAND Looks Better in Lingerie Than I Do ... DAMN IT

"Yes he was," I said. "He told me all about it. How he was a mechanic for some ranking official, how he lived with some woman . . ."

His uncle started laughing, "You must have misunderstood what he was telling you. He was never in the military, but what he told you was how it was for me when I was in Vietnam."

"That can't be right. He told me it was his experience as a mechanic in the military that was the foundation for him opening his own mechanic shop."

His uncle laughed even harder and this time said, "He's never been a mechanic. He held a couple odd jobs here and there but the job he held the longest was as the night janitor at the local K-Mart store. That's all I've ever known of him doing. He got a job at the factory about 10 years ago, but he's never been a mechanic."

"Did his dad own a trucking company?"

"His dad didn't own the company, but his dad ran the office for a trucking company."

"Little Redneck told me he got his CDL license by being grandfathered in to his dad's trucking company. He told me stories about his driving experiences."

By now his uncle had stopped laughing and reached out to take hold of my hand. "Honey, I'm sorry, but none of that is true. Why didn't you say something to us about the things he was telling you?"

"Why would I?" I asked as the tears began to stream down my face. I felt so small. So ashamed of being fooled. So stupid.

Although I had started sessions with Dr. Stith in an attempt to save my marriage, I continued the sessions because of how devastated I was from my experiences of the previous years. I told her about my conversation with Little Redneck's uncle and how stupid I felt for believing everything my husband had told me. I told her how stupid I felt for seeing him in such a brilliant light. I told her how stupid I felt for being so easily deceived. I told her how stupid I felt because even with him dead he was still messing with my head.

"Why would you allow something someone else did make you feel stupid?" she asked. "It's not normal to automatically question the things someone tells us, especially when it's someone we love. Why would you question the things he told you?" Somehow her words made me feel a little less stupid.

I was crushed from the entire experience and began each morning crying – spent most days in bed crying – and went to sleep each night crying. It was difficult for me to even get out of bed because I felt as if I had no purpose in life. I didn't have a job to go to. I was alone and didn't share my home with anyone. I was even fatter now than I had ever been in my life. I figured, what's the use, so I just cried.

I did continue visits to Dr. Stith – but even spent most of my time there crying. She'd ask questions but it would be difficult for me to answer. Not because I didn't have the answers, but because I'd be sobbing uncontrollably. After several visits she said, "You need to get over this and get on with living."

I thought, *"That was pretty harsh. How am I supposed to get on with living? We're right in the middle of the holiday season, I'm alone, and I'm supposed to 'get on' with it? Isn't it obvious that I'm in pain here?"* But I couldn't say anything because I was crying.

Then she continued, "It was him who chose to stop living – you're still alive, but you're not living. In biblical times the period of mourning was 30 days – you're well beyond that time. It's time to dry your tears, open your eyes, and start living again."

This time I thought, *"You know, that really is good advice,"* so that's what I decided to do.

03

THERE'S MORE TO ME THAN I REALIZED

I decided that getting back to living my life was exactly what I needed to do. I looked around to see what pieces of my life I could pick up where I'd left off – before Little Redneck – but found nothing. I had retired so I couldn't throw myself into my work – I had no work. My children were raised and out on their own, so I couldn't put my focus on raising my kids. I no longer had a husband – so I was alone with no one to share my life. I had nothing to go back to, so I had to come up with some way to start a whole new life. But where was I going to start?

Right at the time I was looking for a way to start anew I became a grandmother with the birth of my son's son – the best thing to have happened in my life for years.

Since my whole life had changed, I decided a good place to begin was to have a new place to live. I didn't want to stay in my current house where I could be haunted by so many unhappy memories. I began thinking about what I would like in a house and decided I wanted a big garage with a little house attached. Little Redneck had introduced me to motorcycles, one of the good things that had come from our relationship, and I owned a 2000 Yamaha V-Star 1100. A big garage would give me plenty of room for my car, my motorcycle, and my riding lawn mower. But, since it was only me, I wanted that big garage to be attached to a small ranch style house.

I started looking through the Real Estate section of the local newspaper to see what was available. I'd drive around the various neighborhoods to see what they offered. While looking at houses for sale, I quickly recognized a pattern: if it was a big garage then a big house came with it – usually a split level or two stories. If it was a ranch style house, then there was only a small one car garage. That was just not what I wanted.

I finally saw an ad for a 1400 square foot ranch style house with a two-and-a-half car garage attached – exactly what I wanted – a big garage with a little house attached. I made the appointment to see the house and the moment I walked in I fell in love. I entered the front door into a small entry way with a double-door coat closet on the left. To the right were two bedrooms separated by a bathroom.

From the entry way I stepped into the spacious living room with a cathedral ceiling and a stone fireplace that reached all the way to the top of the ceiling. The double doors at the back of the living room opened onto a deck into the fenced-in yard. As I stepped forward I could see the open kitchen that sat behind the coat closet. *"WOW"*, I thought, *"how open – how spacious – how perfect."* I walked to the left of the living room into the master bedroom suite. There I found a walk in closet, a dressing/make-up room, and a full bath. To the back of the master bedroom were double windows that looked out into the back yard surrounded by a privacy fence. I walked back into the living room and into the kitchen. The utility room was just off the kitchen and had a door leading into the huge garage. I had found what I had been looking for. I just knew it. I told the Real Estate Agent I wanted to make an offer.

"That's great," he said. "But I have to tell you, it's not the current owners, but their mortgage company, who will be accepting any offers because this property is currently in foreclosure proceedings. When you're dealing with foreclosure property it could take several weeks before you will get a response to your offer."

"No problem," I said, but my thoughts were, *"I was a Real Estate Agent for a couple years during the late 1980's, so I know foreclosure proceedings can be both time consuming and costly to the mortgage holder. Sometimes a mortgage holder is willing to take less for the property versus taking the time and expense of continuing the foreclosure proceedings."* On December 30th, 2002, I made an offer on what I believed could possibly be my perfect house.

I showed up at my next session with Dr. Stith full of excitement. I told her about finding my big garage with a little house attached and that I had made an offer to purchase. I was talking so excitedly she could hardly get a word in edgewise. At one point I said, "I wish I was better at decorating. I wish I knew how to choose colors and what styles go with what. I've never been good at anything like that."

"Have you ever looked into taking some decorating classes?" she asked.

"No, I don't want to be a decorator. I just want to be able to do it better."

"That's what I'm talking about," she said, "classes that would just teach you how to be better at decorating. I saw an ad in the paper just today about a local decorator giving such classes. I think I still have that paper in the other room. Do you mind if I go see if I can find it?"

"Sure, no problem."

She left the room but quickly returned with the newspaper. "Here it is. The name of the lady giving the class is Mary Cynthia. The name of her company is 'Decorate by Design.' Here's her contact information." She handed me a piece of paper and a pen so I could write the information down.

"Thanks, I'll check it out and let you know how it goes." Then I said, "Dr. Stith, how long do you think I need to continue coming to see you?"

"That's really up to you. I'm here as long as you need me, or if you think you don't need me anymore, then that's OK too."

"In that case, I think this might just be my last session. I've been much busier lately. I've been getting out more with my friends. As a matter of fact, one of my friends is checking into having weight loss surgery and has asked me to attend a support group meeting with her. I think I might look into the possibilities of having the surgery too. I figure if I'm starting a whole new life, it might as well include a whole new me."

"You seem to be doing much better, but remember, I'm here if you need me."

The next day I called Mary Cynthia and told her I was hoping to buy a new house and was interested in taking her decorating classes. She explained it was rather late for registering for the class, which would begin in a couple days, but, as luck would have it, she had a student cancel and there was a place for me. She and I seemed to immediately develop a friendship from that very first phone conversation. I told her my reasoning for purchasing a new house had stemmed from losing my husband last October. She shared that she had lost a family member about that same time.

After talking for nearly an hour she said, "Bobbie, I feel led to tell you about an event I'm having at my house soon. It's a week-end long workshop. It's not really a religious event, not really a psychic event – I guess it can be best described as more of a spiritual event." Then she laughed and said, "Actually, I just call it 'woo-woo.' It can get pretty intense, but I get the feeling it's something you would find interesting." She told me more about the workshop, time, and location, and she was right – it did sound interesting to me – so I agreed to attend. I told her I was glad she'd had a vacancy in the class and I looked forward to meeting her soon.

I wasn't exactly sure of the location of Mary Cynthia's decorating classes, so I left my house early to make sure I could find it and arrive before class began. The place wasn't as difficult to find as I had thought it might be. Mine was the only car in the parking lot, so I decided to stay in the car and wait for everyone else's arrival. Before long a black SUV pulled into the lot and out stepped a sharply dressed big beautiful woman. She looked to be at least six feet tall, wore vibrant bright colors and had lots of bright red hair. Somehow I knew instantly she was Mary Cynthia. Once inside I introduced myself and we both just seemed to feel like we'd been friends forever and would be for the rest of our lives.

My HUSBAND Looks Better in Lingerie Than I Do ... DAMN IT

I listened intently as she shared information about colors – which ones work together, and which ones don't – textures, and different types of cloth. One tip I especially liked was her discussion on how to decide where to place furniture in a room. "How many of you ladies have ever upset your husband by saying, 'honey, will you put that chair over there for me' just to turn around and say 'no, that doesn't work, put it back?' Well, one little trick that works, and is much easier than moving heavy furniture around, is to lay out your room using paper furniture. Of course, I'm not saying the furniture will actually be paper, but if you use 'graph' paper, and I recommend the one-inch by one-inch grids, then you can place your paper furniture to make sure it fits where you want to put it before calling your husband into the room.

If your room is 12-feet by 14-feet, then use a sheet of graph paper measuring 12-inches by 14-inches to represent the room. Then measure your furniture, and cut pieces of graph paper representing each piece of furniture to be used in the room. For example if you have a foot-stool that is a 2-foot square, then cut a 2-inch square from the graph paper and write 'foot-stool' on that piece of paper. Walla . . . paper furniture. It's much easier to rearrange the paper furniture to get an idea of how everything will fit into the room than it is to get your husband to move furniture only to have to move it again.

I had never thought of doing anything like that before but it made a lot of sense to me. I left her class with many decorating ideas, and a new friend.

The weekend arrived for the 'woo-woo' workshop at Mary Cynthia's. There were approximately 25 people there. The workshop instructors were Bill and Peggy.

The first night consisted of introductions then a short presentation that explained, "We're spiritual beings having a physical experience." I'd never heard it put that way before. I'd been raised in church and had felt the goose bumps when I got lost in prayer or caught up in something the preacher was saying. I had always believed the goose bumps was the evidence that I, as a physical being, was having a spiritual experience. Now, I was being told it was just the other way around. It didn't take me very long to figure out why Mary Cynthia called this stuff woo-woo.

Then Bill said, "And I've brought with me some very powerful, highly sophisticated, scientific equipment to help me make my point. With this equipment you will see evidence you have an energy that extends well beyond your physical body – we'll call it the spiritual you. Not only will you be able to see that there is more to you than what meets the eye, but this highly sophisticated equipment will also show you how your state of mind, your emotions, your thinking, affects your energy."

He had my attention. I was anxious to find out what this 'scientific equipment' was and how it was going to show me there's more to me than just this physical body. Then he brought out his sophisticated scientific equipment – it was two wires that had been cut from a coat hanger and bent into an "L" shape. The smaller end of the "L" had been put through a plastic straw, so that when you hold the straw, the longer end of the "L" moves freely. His highly sophisticated scientific equipment made me laugh.

"You'll pair off with a partner and find a place where you can stand at least six feet from one another. Please try to find a place where you and your partner are the only persons in the room. Each pair of partners will have a set of these highly scientific pieces of equipment to use. First one partner will operate the equipment – or hold one of the "L" shaped wires in each hand by the plastic straw – while the other partner will be the thinker. The thinking partner will choose what to think about – as everyone always does. You'll think about something you classify as good or something you classify as bad. Don't discuss the results of the experiment – or tell what you chose to think about – until we all get back together after we've completed our experiments.

The partner operating the equipment – holding only the plastic straw with both wires pointing in the direction of the thinker – will move slowly toward the thinker. When the wires come into contact with the energy coming from the thinker, they should move – because they have encountered your energy. Make a mental notation of how close or how far apart you are from one another when the wires move. Then the thinker will think again, only this time thinking the opposite category of what they thought previously – either good or bad. Once you have conducted the experiment with one partner being the thinker, then you switch – the thinker now becomes the equipment operator."

I was paired up with a gentleman I had never seen before, and we found the kitchen empty, so that's where we stopped to do our experiment. "Have you ever done anything like this before?" he asked.

"No, I haven't." I answered. "I've been to places where they've taken my aura picture and show different colors all around me. But they had me step on a metal plate or put my hand on a metal plate while the picture was being taken. I just figured that was low frequency electricity coming through my body and they used some sort of special film to capture the electricity by having it show up in different colors. Have you ever done anything like this before?" I asked him.

"Yes, I have, several times, and I'm still always amazed at the results. Do you want to be the operator first or the thinker first."

"I think I'll be the operator first."

"OK," he said, "just step that direction, I'd say at least six feet away, hold loosely onto the plastic straws so the wires can move freely. Give me a minute to center myself and choose my thought. After a couple seconds, start walking slowly in my direction but keep your eye on the wires."

I followed his instructions and got within a foot or so of him and sure enough, as I slowly moved forward the wires moved in opposite directions – the wire in my left hand moved toward the left, and the wire in my right hand moved toward the right – as if I had run into something they couldn't penetrate. I thought, *"I wonder what he did to make those wires move."* Then, as I stopped I said, "They moved at this point. I guess I'm about a foot away from you."

"Good," he said. "Let's do it again and this time I'll think of something else. Again, just give me a couple seconds to center myself and choose a thought."

I went back to my original spot before once again moving toward him with the scientific equipment in my hand. This time the wires separated before I could get within four feet of him. "That's it," I said, "I didn't get as close this time before the wires separated."

"OK, then, it's your turn to be the thinker," he said as I handed him the wires.

Our instruction was to choose to think of something we classified as good or as bad. A bad thought came to me easily – I thought about Little Redneck. My partner started moving slowly toward me. He got so close I believed that if he didn't stop he might poke me with the wires. Then, when he was about six inches away from me, the wires moved. "Ok, now change your thinking," he said, as he moved away from me about four feet or so to start again.

"Change my thinking," I thought. *"Now I need to think about something good. Something good. What in the world can I think about that's good?"* I stood for several minutes trying to come up with a good thought when the good thought finally popped into my head, my grandson, who had just been born in December. I immediately smiled and my experiment partner started toward me, "Oops," he said, "I'm going to have to move back further. The wires have already moved." He turned and walked away from me another couple feet.

I continued thinking about my new grandson and how much pleasure he had brought into my life already – continuing to think of him brought an even broader smile to my face. My experiment partner, now at least six feet away from me, started to take a step forward. "Darn," he said, "I'm going to have to go back even further." This time he stood maybe ten feet away when he turned to walk my direction. "It's like your energy just keeps growing. Every time I turn to come toward you I can't get beyond the first step without the wires moving."

About that time we were called back together with

the others for everyone to share the results of their experiments and what we each had learned. When it was my turn, I shared that I had decided the experiment was a success. It did show me that I put out energy, and my energy is affected by my thoughts because no one but me knew what my thoughts had been. I was amazed at my own energy output results from thinking good or bad thoughts.

I shared that the experiment also told me that sometimes I have to give more effort to finding something good to think about because, for me at least, it seemed to be much easier to think bad thoughts. In conclusion I smiled and added, "I've decided if I ever need to lift my energy, all I have to do is choose to think about my grandson."

Then, speaking to all the workshop attendees Bill said, "I'd like to say something about what Bobbie just said. She said she can 'choose to think about her grandson.' Remember earlier when I gave you the instructions on how to conduct the experiment using my highly sophisticated scientific equipment? If you recall, I said, 'The thinking partner will choose what to think about – as everyone always does.' I know everyone heard the part where I said you will choose what to think about – but did you pick up on the part of my statement where I said, 'as everyone always does?"

As I looked around the room a couple people were shaking their heads as if they had picked up on the 'as everyone always does' statement, but most, including me, were shaking our heads no, we had completely missed the last part of Bill's statement.

He continued by saying, "I want to stress the importance of that statement. YOU ALWAYS HAVE THE

ABILITY TO CHOOSE WHAT YOU THINK ABOUT – no one else can think for you – only you – and we learned through our experiments here today that what we choose to think – whether positive or negative – does make a difference. Now, let's all choose to have a safe trip back to our homes tonight, get plenty of rest, and be here early tomorrow morning."

Early the following morning we gathered back together for our second day of the workshop. I was still reeling from the previous day's exercise and couldn't wait to see what today was going to offer – I just knew it was going to be something wonderful – I could feel the excitement from within.

Soon it was Peggy's turn to guide us in an exercise. First she put us all up against the wall in a line standing side by side. Then she said, "The banquet table called life sits before you. On this table is every good thing your heart has ever desired. Can you imagine the table? What sits on that table for you – what is it that you desire? Everything you've ever desired is right there in front of you. It's always there for you. Oh, you can want what's on that banquet table, and maybe even wish for it, desiring it, craving it. But you're so burdened with the baggage of past experiences your knees are about to buckle under the load. Your feet are frozen in place unable to move because of the weight of your baggage. So the banquet table remains just outside your reach – but it's always there – everything you've ever desired – just out of reach.

Only you have packed the baggage you carry based on your experiences. Only you know what's packed in your baggage. You've filled your baggage with every excuse that stops you from moving forward and experiencing the good the banquet table of life offers – every 'I'm not good enough' or 'It's not my fault' or 'I can't.' What's in your bag of burden? Is it, 'He done me wrong?' Is it, 'Someday when this happens or when that happens then I'll be happy?' What's in the baggage you carry – you should know – you're the one who filled it – you're the one who carries the burden of it.

Then she started walking up and down in front of us as her voice became progressively louder and louder. "Can you feel how large the baggage is that you carry on your back, on your shoulders? Can you feel the weight of the bags you've packed for yourself? Reach behind you. Feel the size of the baggage you're carrying. What's stuffed inside your baggage? You should know what's in your baggage – after all, you're the one who stuffed your bag so full. Reach around, get hold of that baggage. What have you packed away in your heavy heavy bag? What is it that you carry that weights you down so?"

It was easy to imagine the size and weight of my baggage behind me – it was enormous. I sure had a lot packed inside the bag I was carrying filled with the experiences of my past. I started packing my bags way back when I was born an illegitimate child – that alone was enough to put me on the road to 'I'm not good enough.' Then there was being sexually molested by a step-father beginning when I was only five years old and continuing until my mom divorced him when I was ten – there was a lot of shame and guilt pushed way down in the bottom of my bag that came from that experience. On top of those experiences I'd piled the misery of low self-esteem from being so fat – I had more than enough of that packed in my bags. Then there was the pain of a failed marriage – the hell I'd endured with Little Redneck – yep, my bags were full alright, and extremely heavy. I was acutely aware of everything I carried in my baggage because it was all mine – I had experienced every bit of it.

For some reason, when Peggy reached where I was standing she stopped within inches of my face. By this time her face was red and her voice loud as if she were angry. She yelled, "I want to see what's in your bag. Show me. Show me what's in your bag."

I just stopped and looked at her rather stunned for a moment. "It's so important to you that you carry it with you all the time. Show me what's so important to you. What have you got in your bag? Reach around behind you, pull from your bag an example of what's holding you back and let me see it. Show me. Show me."

I went right along with imagining my heavy burden and reached behind me acting as if I had pulled something from my bag. I held out empty hands, palms up, as if to show her what had come from my bag. Peggy slapped my hands down and yelled even louder as she moved even closer to my face. "I don't see anything. What's holding you back Bobbie. Show me what's in your bag."

A second time I reached behind me as if to dig deeper into my bag to reveal my burdens. Again I brought forth empty hands to present to Peggy. Before I could even extend my hands she once again slapped my hands away and screaming loudly said, "I don't see anything. I want to SEE what's holding you back. Show me. SHOW ME WHAT'S BEHIND YOU."

By this time I, too, was angry, my feelings were hurt, and I began to cry as I screamed back, "THERE'S NOTHING BEHIND ME."

She suddenly smiled and softly said, "Exactly. There's nothing behind you to hold you back – no-thing. We only imagine there is. We burden ourselves with our past experiences and allow them to hold us back, but there's really nothing there. No-thing. It's gone. The past is over. It's not there anymore. In order to move forward all we have to do is simply let go – to drop the burdens we impose upon ourselves."

I looked behind me as if I might really find something this time, but I saw NO-THING. I symbolically dropped my heavy heavy baggage and stepped forward – no longer carrying the weight of my past. I immediately felt lighter.

That exercise was quite intense and emotionally draining so we took a short break to enjoy some refreshments and socializing, then Bill called us all back together once again. He began this time by saying, "Now that you have dropped your heavy burdens and know how to move forward in life, where do you want to go? Each of you will decide the answer to that question for yourself, but this next exercise might help you reach your destination. For now, our desire is to get from point 'A' in the room to point 'B' in the room. Everyone line up in single file and as you reach the front of the line it will be your turn. Begin by stating your desire, like this, 'It is my desire to reach point B.'

Once you've stated your desire to reach point B, you will then state how you're going to accomplish getting there. Oh, here's the catch. No two people can get there the same way. Peggy and I will go first to show you what we're talking about."

Bill started the exercise by going to the front of the line and stating, "It is my desire to reach point B and I'm going to get there by walking." Then he simply walked to his desired destination. Next, Peggy stepped up and said, "It is my desire to reach point B and I'm going to accomplish this by running." She then took off running to reach her destination.

"Darn," I thought, *"I wish I were closer to the front of the line before all the good ways to get there are gone."* As I looked around the room I could tell most everyone else was having the same thoughts as me from the looks on their faces and how quiet the room had become. Each one of us 25 or so participants stepped up to take our turn. As each reached the front of the line they announced their desire to reach point B and the decision they'd made on how to get there. One skipped, one crawled, one hopped, one danced, one rowed a boat, one flew like an airplane, and so on and so on.

As I watched I'd have a thought, *"Oh, I can do it this way,'* but then someone else would do it that way which meant I would have to come up with another way. Each time that happened I'd think, *"Crap, I'll never be able to come up with a different way to get there."* But, when it was my turn, I did think of a way to reach my destination that no one else had thought of. As I stepped up to the front of the line I proudly announced, "It is my desire to reach point B and I'm going to get there by riding my motorcycle." I revved up the engine on my imaginary motorcycle, twisted the throttle, and rode to point B.

To my surprise, all 25 or so of us reached our destination, and no two people did it the same way. That's when Bill said, "OK, now let's do it again. As before, we can't repeat any of the ways anyone has already used."

"*No way,*" I thought. "*How can we come up with 25 different ways again?*" But, we did. None of the ways previously used were repeated, and no two ways were alike this round either. Then, a third time Bill said, "Let's do it again, and the same rules apply." However, instead of the sense of dread of having to come up with a different way, an amazing thing began to happen. My mind was flooded with all sorts of ways to cross the room that no one had used yet. There seemed to be endless possibilities. And, the ways the others did use were ways I hadn't even thought of yet. All of a sudden the room was no longer quiet with everyone thinking about how to accomplish their goal, but there was laughter and cheers for the imaginative ways being used.

As the last participant finished the third round Bill said, "This exercise shows us how, when we set our goal, and make it known to the Universe, or in other words, 'let go and let God', then the Universe, or God, or Higher Power, or whatever label you choose to use, joins in helping us reach that goal. How many of you were wondering what you were going to come up with as a different way of reaching your destination in the beginning of the exercise?" All hands in the room were raised.

"By the end of the exercise, how many of you had so many ideas that you could have played another round or two?" Again, all hands in the room were raised. "My point here is: our possibilities are endless. All we have to do is take that first step, no matter how tiny, or silly, or insignificant that first step might seem to us, we just take that very first step toward our hearts desire, our destination, our goal, and then the Universe seems to propel us in the right direction. The steps that lead you there might not take you down the path you expected them to, but that's another exercise.

We call it synchronicity – a meaningful coincidence. When you learn to look for and identify the coincidences, the synchronicity, it's easy to see how each synchronized step is leading you toward your destination. Whether you are consciously aware of it or not, synchronicity is what brought you here, today, to this very workshop. Think back to how you came to be a participant in this workshop. Can you identify the synchronicity – the steps that brought you here?"

Boy, could I readily identify the steps that lead me to this moment. It was Mary Cynthia's invitation. I'd met Mary Cynthia because Dr. Stith shared her contact information from an ad she'd read in the newspaper that day just before I arrived in her office for my appointment. It was in that appointment I shared about making an offer on a house and wanting to learn more about decorating. Synchronicity – meaningful coincidences – all the way.

Before ending the workshop Bill and Peggy introduced us to "Be-Have-Do" which is a 15 minute writing exercise to help begin each day. They explained that Be-Have-Do sets the tone for your day. It helps you to put focus on the things you already have in your life to be grateful for – helps you to bring to light the things you would like to have – and the do list becomes steps you can take to bring the things you would like to have to fruition.

They suggested the best time of day to practice Be-Have-Do is immediately upon waking in the morning.

They taught us the three steps of Be-Have-Do beginning with the first minute writing sentences that begin with, "I am so very grateful to be __ __ __ __," and just fill in the blank. Examples of what we might put in the blanks were healthy, employed, happy, or whatever is appropriate for you. Next, you spend seven minutes writing sentences that again begin with, "I am so very grateful to have __ __ __ __," again filling in the blanks with the things you currently have, AND the things you'd like to have. Fill in the blanks with anything you desire. Examples here were shoes to wear, car to drive, job to go to, all the way up to castle to live in, if that's what you desire to have. Then the last seven minutes you simply make a list of what you would like to do, or accomplish, during the day. This list converts into your daily 'to do' list – whatever it is you hope to do during the day – make the bed, buy a new TV, eat out at a fancy restaurant this evening.

I learned so very much that weekend, but feel one of the most important things I learned is there's more to me than just this physical body – there's more to me than I ever realized. I learned my thoughts, and especially my words, do make a difference in my life. I learned to start looking for and recognizing 'my signs' – the synchronicity that leads me. I came away knowing I'd just built a strong foundation upon which to build the rest of my life.

I immediately began practicing Be-Have-Do just as Bill and Peggy had taught. Each morning I'd begin my day by setting the timer on my microwave to do my Be-Have-Do morning writing. From the workshop I'd also learned about journaling. One of the benefits of journaling is that later when you go back to read the journal, you can see the synchronicity that brought you to where you are today. So, I'd start my days writing Be-Have-Do and end my days by writing in a journal. It took only a couple weeks of doing my daily writing before I began to see a big difference in my attitude, and my life.

Various things – people, books, movies, experiences – started showing up in my life that reiterated what Bill and Peggy had taught. I began calling them God's 'stepping stones' because each leads me to the next 'stepping stone' which takes me to the next, and so on. I see them as God's way – the way of my higher self – leading where my life is supposed to take me.

One of my first 'signs' or 'stepping stones' was a tiny little book, *The Hidden Messages In Water,* by Masaru Emoto. The book is about an experiment which uses words with water, and the results of 'mixing' the two. I was absolutely blown away by what it had to say about the words we choose to use – especially about the negative self-talk we all do, and the words we say to our children. I think what made me realize the importance of using positive words in our self-talk and toward our children is when the book pointed out we 'physical beings,' are made mostly of water.

Not long after I attended the workshop Alan called again. "I'm just checking in on you to see how things are going," he said.

"Actually, I'm doing better than I was the last time we talked. Remember calling me when you saw Little Redneck's obituary?"

"Yes, I remember. You were pretty shook up so I figured that wasn't the time to talk. I was afraid you'd just think I was trying to get back in your bed. And that's not the reason for this call either. I'm genuinely concerned and want to let you know I'm here if you need anything."

"I appreciate that. It is quite an adjustment to make. No more job. Living alone. No one to love. I think that's what concerns me the most – the no one to love part. I can't imagine ever falling in love like that again."

"It'll happen. You'll fall in love again. You'll never experience love like you've had in the past because a new love will be different. No two loves are alike. And no one love is better than another – they're all love – and they're all different."

I smiled a little as I said, "I hope you're right."

"Mark my words. I'm right," he said, and I could almost sense a smile on his face too.

We chatted a few minutes longer and after we hung up I thought, *"I sure hope he knows what he's talking about."*

04

STARTING OVER

I had made the offer on the big garage with the little house attached in December of 2002. The Real Estate Agent had told me it could take some time before I might receive a response, and he was right. It was early April 2003 when my offer to purchase was finally accepted. Once my offer to purchase was accepted I was given access to the property even before the closing. To make it truly 'mine,' there were some things I wanted to do to the new house – paint all the rooms; install new carpet in the bedrooms and living room; install new flooring in the entryway, bathrooms, and kitchen; update the ceiling fans and light fixtures throughout the house; install French doors in the living room leading out onto the deck, install a door with etched glass for the front of the house, and install new appliances in the kitchen. Since my old house hadn't sold yet it worked out well that I could remain living in my old house while making the repairs and upgrades to the new house. On July 4, 2003 weekend my family and friends helped me move into my perfect new house – even though I didn't close on the property until July 11. It was an easy move because

I had decided that since I was building a whole new life, there wasn't much I wanted to keep from my old life, so I either sold or gave away most of my old furniture and home décor instead of bringing it to the new house. The largest objects moved were my washer and dryer.

I set up my computer and office desk in the back bedroom on the side of the house where the two bedrooms are separated by a bathroom. The front bedroom on that side of the house, my guest bedroom, was empty, but I did at least put towels and a roll of toilet paper in the guest bathroom. Across the living room to the other side of the house, in my bedroom, I had only a bed, a small TV I sat on the chest of drawers, and the rocking chair her dad bought on the day we brought our daughter home from the hospital when she was born. Instead of having a kitchen table, I had a bar custom built between the kitchen and living room – which separated the rooms while maintaining the openness. The furniture in my living room was an old pedal-foot Singer sewing machine and four Shaker chairs, the type with thatched bottoms, all of which had once belonged to my grandmother.

There wasn't a great deal of life insurance money left after paying the funeral expenses for Little Redneck, and with all the home improvements, it didn't take me long to spend most of the money I did have. Of course, the suicide of Little Redneck eliminated over half the household income I'd grown accustomed to having, and my early retirement meant I wasn't bringing home nearly as much as I did when I was on the job either. I'd lost approximately 75% of our combined income. I was thankful to have my beautiful perfect little house to show for the money I'd spent, but was concerned as to how I was going to be able to make two house payments until I could sell my old house.

I decided to do what I had learned in the workshop at Mary Cynthia's. I made it known to the Universe – what I know as praying to God – that I needed to sell my old house, then I let go to let God take care of getting it done. I found that when I 'let go and let God' somehow things do work out. When I think, *"I have no idea how I'm going to pay my bills this month,"* I continue that thought with, *"but, I know they will get paid,"* and they always do.

Every time I'd have thoughts about doubting that I could come up with the money to make two house payments I'd feel anxious and begin to worry. Then I'd say to myself, "things are what they are so I let go to let God" and I'd consciously choose to change my thoughts to something else – I usually chose to think of my grandson. Once I'd changed my thinking, within a matter of seconds that heavy, gnawing in the pit of my stomach would disappear.

It wasn't always easy to keep my focus on positive thoughts because the worry of being unable to make two house payments would drift right back into my thinking. Usually, I wouldn't even recognize I had drifted back into the dark side, the *'I can't'* thoughts, until my body would begin to feel the heavy, gnawing, anxious feelings again. Once I recognized my thoughts had drifted back to the dark side, I'd shake my head, as if to shake out the *'I can't'* thoughts, and again consciously choose a positive subject matter to think about.

Consciously choosing to change my thinking to a positive subject never changed my situation – I still had two house payments to make. But what it did change was how I was feeling at that moment – consciously choosing a positive thought always made me feel better and eliminated that gnawing in the pit of my stomach feeling. Thinking of my grandson or my children always makes me smile.

Of course, having the negative 'I can't' thoughts never changed my situation either – I still had two house payments to make – no matter what I choose to think about – and I always have the ability to choose my thoughts – to me the true definition of 'God given free will.' What thinking the negative thoughts did do, however, was to make me feel horrible. Before long, it became easier and easier for me to more quickly recognize when I'd drifted to the dark side. I don't like feeling anxious, worried, or upset so within a matter of seconds I'd make the decision to consciously choose thoughts that make me feel better. After a while I realized that my thoughts remain positive most of the time – I no longer have to 'consciously choose' to think positively, it seems to be a natural state of mind for me – most of the time.

Soon after moving into my new house I recognized another stepping stone that crossed my life's path – purchasing "Get the Edge" by Anthony Robbins – a CD series. In the CD's he gives instructions on practices that lead you to your 'edge.' The one thing that remained with me is his 15-minutes to fulfillment, 30-minutes to thrive, or an hour to power scenario. He gives instructions on walking practices. His instructions include certain rhythms, breathing exercises, pressure points, and affirmations.

I still weighted over 250 pounds, so my walk turned out to be the 15-minutes to fulfillment. Two of his suggested affirmations were, "Every day in every way my life gets better and better," or "I love my life." Neither of these set well with me because I couldn't believe either one. Since I wasn't able to come up with an affirmation of my own, I 'convinced' myself that 'every day in every way my life gets better and better.' It took quite a bit of self-talk to get me to believe those words. I thought, *"OK, Bobbie, every day something 'good' happens to you – and when just one good thing happens, then your whole life seems better. Having your new house is a good thing. Getting to decorate it the way you want is a good thing."* That I **could** believe, so as I walked using the rhythms, breathing patterns, and pressure points I'd say to myself 'every day in every way my life gets better and better.' To my surprise, in about a month of saying that affirmation, I realized one day somehow my outlook on life had changed. I loved my life . . . so I changed my affirmation to 'I love my life.'

With a new house that was basically empty I was open to all possibilities, but had no idea as to how I wanted to furnish and decorate my house. I vowed to never allow myself to become lonely or bored, so, on those rare occasions I did feel boredom rear its ugly head, instead of just sitting in an empty house all by myself, I'd often go out shopping, even if it were only window shopping at the local K-Mart store.

It was on one such afternoon when I was in the K-Mart store that I looked up and saw Alan coming down the hallway toward me. It brought a smile to my face, but it also instantly brought a not so good memory of the last time I'd run into Alan at the K-Mart store back when Little Redneck and I had been there together shopping. On the previous occasion I had looked up to see Alan and Mary coming down the hallway toward us, only back then I couldn't smile, but had quickly lowered my head, hoping they hadn't seen us. But, they had seen us and were coming over to us to say hello. I knew how jealous Little Redneck was and how he reacted if I even as much as made eye contact with another man, so I immediately reached out to take his hand and move closer to him. To me, it was like a dog marking his territory, only Little Redneck was the dog and I was his territory. My ploy failed. Alan and Mary stopped just long enough to say hello, then we all continued with our shopping. The whole encounter had taken only a little more than a minute, but as soon as we stepped outside the store Little Redneck started his, "how long have you been fucking him behind my back" accusations and I endured another night of anger and rage.

 I shook the old memories from my mind as Alan approached and I realized that this time I didn't have to be afraid – this time I reached out and gave him a hug and he hugged me back.

 "How are you doing?" he said. "It seems like it's been forever since we've gotten to talk. So, what are you doing these days?"

 "You know I retired last September, don't you? I retired just one month before...," but before I could continue saying anything Alan spoke up and cut me off, as if he didn't want to hear about what happened just a month after my retirement.

 "Yeah, I heard. Bobbie, I'm so very sorry for what you've been through and that your husband..." only this time it was my turn to cut him off by saying, "Can you believe it's been nearly a year ago – well, it's been 10 months actually, but that's nearly a year. Life with him was one hell of an experience, but all that is in the past, so there's no sense in talking about it now. I've moved on with my life and made lots of changes. For one thing I changed my last name back to Thompson. I just couldn't imagine living the rest of my life with his last name. I've also changed where I live – I bought a new house."

"Mary and I bought a new house too, about three months ago. It's just four doors down from mom and dad's house."

"Actually, I made the offer on my house in December of last year, but I didn't get to move in until last month, over July 4th weekend. I still haven't sold my other house yet, but hopefully I will soon. I wanted a big garage with a little house attached, and that's exactly what I got – a two-and-a-half car garage attached to a 1400 square foot ranch."

I heard the small-talk words coming out of my mouth, but what I really wanted to say was, "I'd like for us to get together" but instead I looked up at him, giving away my thoughts because I was unable to hold back the big smile on my face, as I said, "Would you like to see my new house? I don't have any living room furniture to sit on, so I guess we'd have to sit on the bed."

He instantly smiled back, looked at his watch, and said, "Sure, I've got a few minutes, or hours," and off we went, to *see* my new house.

I was glad that Alan was one of the things from my old life that had moved into my new life. Although we had rekindled our relationship, I wondered just when we were going to be able to see one another. I was really busy. In addition to working on my new house and trying to sell my old house, I was continuing to take night classes at Kentucky State University (KSU) two nights a week working toward a BS in Business Administration – something I'd started doing in the early 1990's. In addition, I'd managed to explore the possibility of having bariatric – or weight loss – surgery. My insurance company finally approved, and on September 29, 2003, I had gastric bypass.

Dr. Weiss and Dr. Oldham with Bluegrass Bariatrics were my doctors. It went wonderfully. I had the RNY gastric bypass, my gall bladder removed, and a hernia repaired – all in one operation – all done laparoscopic. They rolled me into the operating room around 3:30 in the afternoon, and around 10:00 that night they got me out of the bed for the first time – I took my first steps toward a new me.

I finally closed on my old house just two weeks after my surgery – October 15, 2003. I spent the holiday season with my family, like most families do during the holidays, eating. Or, in my case since I'd just had weight loss surgery (WLS), I could only watch as everyone else ate. The WLS had taken the size of my stomach from about the size of a football to about the size of a baseball. A stomach the size of a baseball doesn't hold much food. I could eat anything I wanted, just not very much of it. I filled my plate with one baby-spoon full of each of the foods I liked, but then could eat only about half of what was on my plate. I was thankful that during the few short months since my surgery I'd already lost quite a bit of weight, but I began to question my timing to have WLS just prior to the holiday season.

During most of 2004 my main focus was finishing my degree and slowly pulling my house together. I spent most of my free time going to WLS support group meetings, going on motorcycle rides with a couple different motorcycle groups I'd joined, and occasionally dating. It was one of the guys I dated very briefly who brought me my next recognized stepping stone – a book entitled *"The Celestine Prophecy"* by James Redfield. It is fiction, but it somehow opened my mind to possibilities I'd never before imagined.

I don't think I would have had an open mind to enjoy the possibilities presented in the book if I hadn't recently taken a particular class at KSU. I needed an elective so I chose something called "Foundations of Culture." On our first night of class for Foundations, the professor presented the book of Genesis from the bible and talked about how 'God spoke' the world into existence then made man, Adam, from the dirt then eventually made woman, Eve, from Adam's rib. My thoughts were, *"How in the world is a state school getting away with teaching a bible class?"*

Then I heard something I'd never in my life ever heard before when the professor mentioned Adam's FIRST wife, Lilith.

"Do what?" I thought, *"Where did that come from."* He told us about certain texts that say when God made Adam – a man – from the earth, he also made Lilith – a woman – from the earth at the same time. Equals. But when Adam wanted Lilith to be his subordinate she refused because she had been made "in the likeness of God" just as Adam had been and struck out on her own to keep from being under his rule. That's when Adam

asked for a subordinate woman, thus, Eve was made from his rib. *"Blasphemy,"* I thought. When I got home from class that night I went straight to the internet to research Lilith, and, sure enough, I found her, or at least information about her.

Our next foundations class was on some culture that believed man came into existence when the ocean spit out a giant female goddess and as she approached dry land she shook her wet hair to get it out of her face. As the drops of mud in her hair from the ocean's depths were flung to the ground, the drops became men and women. When I heard that tale I immediately thought, *"How stupid is that?"* Then, as if to answer my own question on the level of stupidity of that story I instantly had the thought, *"Really, I bet it's not 'stupid' to the people who have been taught all their lives that's the way mankind was created. What if you said to them; 'God made Eve from Adam's rib, and then Mary, a virgin, gave birth to God's son, Jesus.' Think they might call your story 'stupid?"* By the time my "Foundations in Culture" class had ended I realized there was a lot more to this world than I knew about. I came away from that class much more open minded.

It was during that semester, around mid-October when my sister, Mitzi, ran into an old friend of ours, Chiquita. We had known Chiquita some twenty-five or so years ago when she had been married to our step-brother. During their brief encounter, Mitzi learned that Chiquita was now single. She told Chiquita that I, too, was single and searching for a friend to go out and do things with. Chiquita gave Mitzi her phone number and asked her to tell me to give her a call.

I did call and it was wonderful to chat with her after so many years. After catching up a bit, I told her how I enjoyed partying at Jim Porter's Good Time Emporium in Louisville and invited her to go with me to attend one of their most popular nights, Halloween. She agreed to go with me, and I was so excited about the opportunity to get to see her again.

A few days later after reconnecting with Chiquita I was on my way to my first cruise – a Caribbean Cruise. Patients from the hospital where I had my weight loss surgery had started a social group and had orchestrated the whole thing for the week of October 17-23, 2004. It was while on the cruise I met Vallarie and instantly loved her. Vallarie is a little taller than me, blond hair, big breasts, and what I lovingly refer to as my 'trashy' friend. Not that she's trashy, but she sure does like wearing the makeup – especially eye shadow. I think of her as my 'trashy' friend because she reminds me of that country song that says, "I like my women just a little on the trashy side. Where they wear their clothes too tight and their hair is dyed – too much lipstick and too much rouge." Yep, that's my girly girl Vallarie.

The week after returning home from the cruise I got a phone call from Alan. He said he was in the neighborhood, but, living in such a small town, anywhere in town is 'in the neighborhood.' I laughed and said, "Well, since you're in the neighborhood anyway, do you have time to stop by the house?"

He replied with, "I was hoping that's what you'd say. I'll be there in just a minute."

I hadn't had the opportunity to see Alan for nearly a year. Although we'd spoken on the phone, and even that was rare, we hadn't seen one another since I'd had the weight loss surgery. I couldn't wait to see him, because by this time I'd lost nearly 100 pounds and was feeling wonderful. I barely had time to hang up the phone when my doorbell rang. As I opened the door I posed for him, running my hands down my sides to emphasize my still large breasts and my now much smaller waistline, then twisted my hips in his direction as I asked, "You like?"

"WOW," he said, "You look wonderful."

"Thanks," I said, pleased that he liked what he saw.

Our sex life together had always been good, but this was the first time we'd had sex since I'd lost weight. I was astonished at how much more energy I had and how much more flexible I was. *"Wow,"* I thought, *"I'd had weight loss surgery a long time ago if I'd known this would be one of the perks."*

A few days later I was summonsed to my door by the ringing of the bell once again. This time there was a beautiful witch at my door – Chiquita. I had always thought Chiquita was one of the most beautiful women I'd ever seen. She has American Indian heritage and you can tell by looking – dark hair, dark skin, and piercing green eyes. Even the witch's costume she had chosen for the party made her look beautiful. It was black with a large orange feather on the witch's hat, an orange belt at her waist, and orange feather cuffs at the end of the sleeves. I decided to be Mae West – incognito, of course. I'd found a royal blue sequined gown at Goodwill and added a feather boa and a feathered mask that covered half my face. We had the best time that evening.

The following weekend we three girls, Chiquita, Vallarie, and I, got together for the first time to go out dancing. We all love dancing, and flirting with the guys.

My HUSBAND Looks Better in Lingerie Than I Do ... DAMN IT

Bobbie in 2003, a few months prior to undergoing weight loss surgery.

Bobbie in 2013

We immediately become the new 3-Muskateers. Before long, when you would see one of us, you'd see the three of us together.

I finally graduated from college in December 2004 – six months after my baby girl had graduated from college – I was 49 years old. Mitzi decided to give me a graduation party on January 15, 2005. I was so happy. Life was wonderful. I loved my new house, I loved my new size, I loved being a college graduate, I loved having so many family members and friends come celebrate my graduation, and I loved having Chiquita and Vallarie to run around with. I loved my life.

I was at Mitzi's a few days later thanking her for such a wonderful party and said, "You know, for months after Little Redneck died I never thought I would ever be able to say I love my life, but, I LOVE MY LIFE. I guess Tony Robbins' affirmation – I love my life – works."

"What are you talking about?" she asked. Then I told her about the Get the Edge CD's and the affirmation. She responded by saying, "Bullshit, just saying, 'I love my life' ain't going to make your life any better."

"Maybe it does, Mitzi." I shot back at her. "I have no idea HOW it works, but, for me at least, it has worked. When I first began doing the affirmation I wondered just what I did have in life to love. I weighed over 250 pounds, I no longer had a job, and I was alone because my husband had just committed suicide. Now, I have a new home, am much healthier after having lost 100 pounds, and have wonderful family and friends who love me as you well know from the turnout at the graduation party – life is good – I love my life."

"Your life may be good, but just saying 'I love my life' didn't make it that way."

"You know, Mitzi, I read someplace where someone asked the question, 'If I told you the way to happiness in life is to begin every morning, before your feet even touch the floor, by thinking about the things you have to be grateful for – would you be willing to give it a try – or would you just say, 'bullshit, that's too simple' – and never even give it a try?' I get the feeling you'd be one of those people who would say 'that's too simple' and never even try."

"You're probably right," she said, so I just dropped the subject.

A couple months later I was on the phone with Mitzi talking about first one thing then another when she suddenly said, "Oh, have you heard about Alan?"

The way she had asked the question I just knew something terrible had happened to him. He's known for driving recklessly so fear ran through me as I expected her next words to be, "He got killed in a car wreck last night" or something to that effect. I swallowed hard trying not to let my feelings show, yet my voice was shaking as I replied, "No, what about Alan?"

She was apparently unaware of my reaction to her question and quickly said, "He thinks he's a girl. He's decided he wants to have a sex change operation."

"At least he's not dead," I thought as silently I let out a sigh of relief. Then my next thought was, *"best damn dick around and he wants to cut it off – what a waste."*

"Really?" I responded unable to hold back my surprise. I wanted to say, "The last time we were together he never mentioned anything like that to me," but I couldn't let her know anything about the history Alan and I shared.

It was a warm mid-summer day, a couple months after my conversation with Mitzi about Alan wanting to be a girl, when I was once again at the local K-Mart store and looked up just in time to see Alan standing a couple aisles over from where I stood. Only, this time, I didn't hurry over to give him a hug, but quickly ducked out of sight hoping he hadn't seen me. What I saw shocked me. He looked horrible. His hair was thinning and looked as if he had bleached it to an extreme blond. His face was pale and sallow and his mannerisms confirmed what Mitzi had said, 'he thinks he's a girl.' I quickly left the store eliminating any possibility of us talking. A couple weeks later I heard he'd changed his name to Alana.

Just a few weeks after seeing Alan and being shocked by his appearance, I was driving down the road in my car when my cell phone rang – it was him calling. I hesitated for a moment, but decided to answer.

"Bobbie, this is Alan," he said, "I've got some not so good news I need to share with you."

"This is it," I thought, *"he's finally going to get around to telling me he wants to be a girl."* Then I said, "Give me a second, I'm driving, let me pull over." I pulled my car off the road at the first available spot I came to then went back to my phone. "OK, I've stopped – now what's your news?"

Without any hesitation he just blurted out the words, "I've been diagnosed with HIV."

I gasped from the shock of his words and it was difficult to hold back the tears as I repeated, "HIV?" The only thing I knew about HIV was that it leads to AIDS – and death.

I was trying hard not to cry as he said, "It's not as bad as it sounds. They tell me that having HIV is not the same as having AIDS and it doesn't have to lead to AIDS. I'll be OK." Then he brought up Magic Johnson and how long it had been since he had been diagnosed with HIV. "I wish I could have kept this from you, but, since you and I have had sex together, you need to go get tested."

I didn't want Alan to know I was trying not to cry, so I swallowed hard and said "I do get tested and have done so ever since Little Redneck died. I'm OK."

I knew I was OK because at my very first gynecology appointment after Little Redneck's death my doctor asked if I wanted to be checked for sexually transmitted diseases. "I haven't been with anyone." I told her. But she said, "You just told me you learned your husband was cheating, he could have brought something home to you." That was a possibility that had never crossed my mind.

Then Alan said, "Well, it's good to know that you get tested, and a load off my mind. I'll let you get back to your driving."

I was only able to squeak out the word, "OK" as I choked backed the tears and hung up the phone and the emotions came flooding in. I don't know how long I sat there in the car crying before I finally looked up – I was sitting just two blocks away from Alan's house. I quickly turned my car around and went home – distraught and unfit for accomplishing anything that day.

For the remainder of 2005 my attention was on running around with my friends. Every weekend Chiquita, Vallarie, and I were out dancing. Vallarie and I would start on Thursday nights. Vallarie would pack a bag for the weekend and head to my house after she got off from work. We'd get dressed then head to Lexington to Horseshoes, a country bar where Thursday nights is 'ladies night.' We'd get in free, and ladies drinks were only 75-cents.

On Friday I'd sleep late but Vallarie would get up to go to work. Then she'd usually take a nap when she got back to my house after work. We'd get ready and head out to pick up Chiquita, decide which one of the local bands we wanted to dance to, and then party the night away. After closing down the bars, we'd head to one of the local all-night restaurants for breakfast before heading to the house and sleep most of the day away on Saturday only to do it all over again on Saturday night.

Both Chiquita and Vallarie worked, but not me since I was retired. While they worked I spent much of my time reading and watching TV. I flipped on the TV one day to the local PBS channel and they were having their yearly fund raising telethon. I was instantly mesmerized by the speaker, Dr. Wayne Dyer. I made a donation to the PBS station so I could get the materials he was offering. From listening to the CD's and reading his book called, "The Power of Intention" I was lead to Louise Hay and her video "You Can Heal Your Life" I soon began enjoying Hay House Radio on my computer.

I loved my life, but I lived on only my small retirement income. Soon running around three nights every weekend was costing me more than I was making. My credit card balances started to climb and I was enjoying our festive weekends too much to stop, so I decided it was time for me to find a job. After unsuccessfully looking for something for a couple months I finally found a temporary full-time position at the University of Kentucky in March 2006.

I hadn't been working long when I got another phone call from Alan, "Hey, guess where I am?" he asked.

"I have no idea," I answered.

"I'm on the road learning how to drive an 18-wheeler."

"You're doing what?"

"I decided I needed a career change, so right after Christmas I started truck driving school. I'm doing my hands-on driving training right now. I've already gotten to see a lot of the country and every now and then I'll see something that makes me think of you. I just had you on my mind so I decided to give you a call."

I listened as he did most of the talking telling me about some of the sights he'd seen driving cross country. He sounded upbeat and happy and I felt happy for him. After a while he said, "Well, we're getting ready to stop up here for a bit then it will be my turn to take over the wheel, guess I'd better say goodbye."

I smiled as we hung up because he sounded so happy. Not once did he mention anything about changing his name to Alana or about wanting to be a girl. My thought was, *"truck driving – now that's a man's job – guess he got over that girl crap. Must have been just a passing phase he was going through. I guess that's why he's never said anything to me about it. "*

About a month later there was a knock at my door. I opened the door to find Alan standing there. He looked like his old self again – nothing like the pale bleached blond I'd seen in the K-Mart store. "Howdy," he said.

"Well, howdy," I replied as he entered the door.

"I hope you don't mind me just stopping by like this. I have a few days at home before I get back on the road again. Just thought I'd stop by a few minutes to see how you're doing."

"Sure, no problem, come on in."

We sat on the couch together as he told me about some of the places he'd been. As had happened every other time we ever found ourselves alone together, we both began to feel that extreme sexual energy between us. He reached over and kissed me.

"Can we do this?" I questioned. "We haven't been together since you told me you were diagnosed with HIV."

"Yes, we CAN do this," he answered, "but you have to decide if you WANT to do this. We just have to be careful, use protection, and there are certain things we shouldn't do." He told me how when he was first diagnosed with HIV he thought he'd never be able to have sex again and how he'd gone about disinfecting everything he touched. But since that time he'd learned more about the disease itself and what steps and precautions to take to be able to continue to not only have a sex life, but to live life itself. "So, do you WANT to do this?" he asked.

I answered his question by taking his hand, leading him into the bedroom, opening the top drawer of my nightstand, and handing him a box of condoms.

When he left that day I thought, *"Yep, I was right. That girl stuff must have been just a passing phase because he was all man here today – just like he's always been."*

My focus for the rest of the year was working, partying on the weekends with Chiquita and Vallarie, and recognizing my stepping stones. The next stepping stone turned out to be the movie The Secret – the version with Esther Hicks. There was just something about Esther Hicks that intrigued me. Monday thru Wednesday I'd work, come home in the evenings, grab a quick bite to eat, read for a while, and go to bed early – then I'd party hardy from Thursday thru Sunday morning.

I'd been working in my temporary position at UK for nearly nine months, and the extra income had put me in a position to be able to refinance my house. I paid off all my bills, including the credit cards, which left me with nothing but a house payment. I wanted to continue having some form of income, but, after having been retired since the end of 2002, I decided that being tied down to a desk again was no longer to my liking.

I had a friend who lived in Louisville, Lydia, who was a Mortgage Broker and asked me if I'd like to start the New Year with a new career by joining her office as a mortgage loan originator. She explained I would no longer be tied to a desk, and since I have a rather outgoing personality, I would be good at the job. I'd heard mortgage loan originators could make good money and having freedom again sounded good to me. I told her I'd give it some consideration.

05

FREAKED OUT

In mid-December 2006 I was sitting at my computer when I got an instant message on my screen. It was Alan. "Hey," he said, "what'cha doin?"

"Just checking my e-mails real quick before I head out to go to the mall to do some Christmas shopping," I replied.

"Mom and I are planning on going to the mall later too, but we're watching a UK basketball game right now. It would be nice if we could go to the mall together."

"Yeah," I typed, "but I don't want to wait until after the game to go, I'm getting ready to leave now. You can go with me, but you'll have to miss the game."

"That's OK with me; I don't think mom was really looking forward to getting into the shopping crowd anyway. I'm the one who really needs to go to the mall, and I don't mind missing the game. Can you come pick me up at mom's?"

"Sure," I said, "I'm leaving my house right now. I'll be there in just a minute."

I shut down the IM, grabbed my coat, and headed out the door. I hadn't seen Alan since he'd stopped by my house when he was in for a short stay between trucking runs. I immediately wondered if we could have some 'together' time after our shopping.

I drove over to his mom's and what came bounding out the front door was NOT what I expected – it was a girl – or rather it was a guy trying to look like a girl – but it wasn't Alan. I'd heard the rumors that he wanted to be a girl, and I'd heard he'd changed his name to Alana, but Alan had never once mentioned any of it to me. I thought this girl stuff had all been just a phase. I couldn't believe what I was seeing. His hair was combed to the side resembling a feminine style. He was wearing tight jeans and his nails were long and polished light pink. To me he looked like he could be an escaped mental patient – some of him looked like a man – and some of him looked like a woman – and all of him just looked bizarre.

"Oh my God," I thought. My brain started running out of control as my concerns quickly became all about me being seen with '**THIS**,' *"Crap, now what am I supposed to do? I don't want to be seen in public with THIS lunatic. How am I going to walk through the mall where everyone will see me with this freak-a-zoid?"*

He got into my car and I couldn't even bring myself to look in his direction. I was trapped. I'd already told him he could go to the mall with me, but I didn't know this freak was who I'd be walking through the mall with. I backed my car out of the driveway and headed toward Lexington. Along the way we carried on a polite insignificant conversation but there was absolutely no chemistry between me and the person sitting next to me. This person was in no way Alan – my friend, my lover, the masculine aggressive man I'd compared other men to.

Even as I was pulling into the parking space at the mall I was still thinking, *"How the hell can I go through with this. How can I be seen in public with this person? People will think I'm some sort of nut job just by being in the company of this freak."* Then it dawned on me – this **person** sitting next to me was still a **person**. I thought to myself, *"OK, Bobbie, you know this person, you've known this person for years, you've cared about this person, this person is your friend, this is a good person. You don't know the people at the mall, they don't mean anything to you but your friend does. Just don't pay any attention to anyone else – keep your focus on your friend."*

I'd found it difficult to look in his direction the entire ride to the mall, but once inside, I did nothing but look toward him. I wanted to avoid the faces of everyone around us. I didn't want to see the expressions on their faces if they were thinking Alan was a freak-a-zoid – like I did.

I began paying more attention to what Alan was saying and threw myself into our conversation. Paying attention to carrying on a conversation took my mind off wondering who might be looking at us. I began enjoying our conversation together and was surprised to find 'she' was also a nice person with a quick sense of humor and enjoyable to be around – just like Alan. Before long I was enjoying her jokes, comfortable with our conversation, and realized I was making a new friend.

Once we finished our shopping we decided to stop in the food court for a snack. As we sat across the small table from one another it was quite obvious that Alana was beginning to flirt with me. "You're so cute," she girlishly taunted pointing a finger at me with its perfectly polished nail.

All of a sudden I was uncomfortable again. "Look," I said sternly, "let's get something straight right here and now. I want to make it perfectly clear to you that I can be your 'friend,' because I can be friends with anyone. But that's all we can ever be, 'just friends.' There's no way in hell you and I can ever have the type of relationship that Alan and I had. In all honesty, you already have a strike against you because when you're here you take Alan away from me, and it's Alan that I have a relationship with – not you."

Within my own brain I identified Alan and Alana as two separate entities – one male, and one female. I'd heard about 'split personalities' from that movie that was so popular many years ago, "Sybil" where Sally Fields plays the starring role. I understood Alan and Alana as being two separate personalities – two separate entities.

You could tell the words I said hurt Alana's feelings, but I couldn't help it. That's the way I felt – that's just the way it is and that's that. All of a sudden our being together became strained once again. We quickly finished eating with little talking and headed home. The ride home was almost as uncomfortable for us as the ride to the mall had been. As we approached Versailles Alana said, "Take me back to mom's house."

"I don't mind taking you home," I said.

"Mom's house is my home," she answered. "I've been living there for several months now. Mary and I are separated."

"Do WHAT?" I almost shouted. "You're separated and you never told me?"

"What the hell was I supposed to say Bobbie? I'm single now, but guess what; I'm really a woman in a man's body?"

I again found myself swallowing hard and choking back tears as I pulled into the driveway. As Alana stepped out of the car door I opened my door and stepped out as well. We met in front of the car. I gave her a brief hug as she pecked a good-bye kiss on my cheek and quickly ran toward the house. I barely made it back into my car before the sobbing began. I felt the pain of grief all over again – exactly like the shock I'd felt when that cop said to me, "Mam, your husband is dead. It looks like he's taken his own life." To me, it was if I had just learned that Alan was dead. I went home and cried for hours.

06

STARTING OVER - AGAIN

Just before the end of 2006 I turned in my resignation at the University of Kentucky. I wasn't sure what I wanted to do in the way of earning an income, but I was sure I did not want to continue to be tied to a desk. I decided to take my friend, Lydia, up on her offer to become a mortgage loan originator. We talked and she suggested I begin my training on January 9, 2007. After having worked behind a desk for the previous nine or ten months, a couple weeks of no work sounded good to me.

On Sunday, January 7, I was once again at my computer when an IM from Alan popped up on my screen. It simply said, "Hi"

I didn't know whether or not I should respond. Then I thought, *"Bobbie, the person behind that 'Hi' has been your friend for the better part of your life and a wonderful lover. The least you can do is respond."* So I typed "Hi" back.

Almost immediately the next message popped up, "I really would like to talk to you. We've been friends for a long time and right now I could sure use a friend to talk to. Do you think I could come over?"

Again I hesitated not knowing exactly how to respond. He was right; we had been friends for a long time and had shared a lot together. I felt bad saying no to Alan, but, then again, I didn't want to have to deal with Alana either. I was torn between what to do – be there for my friend, or just throw everything out the window for fear of having to deal with Alana. Finally I typed, "ALAN can come over any time."

The response was, "I'm on my way, but no promises as to who shows up."

I was nervous as I waited for my doorbell to ring. It took only a couple minutes before my wait was over. As I opened the door my eyes lit up and I couldn't hold back a smile. There stood ALAN in all his masculine glory. An air of the masculine aggressiveness was all about him. As he stepped into the room I felt his arm go around my waist. He pulled me against him and kissed me. It was wonderful. That same sexual energy that Alan and I had always shared was present – intensified.

One of my favorite songs is "Into the Night" by Benny Mardones. Every time I hear that song I'm carried away by the words, "If I could fly I'd pick you up, I'd take you into the night, and show you a love, like you've never seen, ever seen." That's exactly what Alan did for me that night – he picked me up and we flew – together we soared to heights I'd never reached before.

I spent most of the next day thanking God that I'd had the opportunity to have closure with Alan – unlike with Little Redneck. I assumed the wonderful night we'd spent together was just God's way of helping me let go of Alan. I assumed incorrectly. Around 2:00 o'clock that afternoon I got a call from Alan. This time I answered with a smile on my face. He said, "You know, we still haven't taken time to talk. I have to leave for work here in a bit, but can I come over when I get off work tonight? I get off at 11:00 p.m."

"Sure," I immediately responded. I knew I had to drive to Louisville to Lydia's office the next morning for my first day on my new job, but I didn't have to be there until 10:00 a.m. I figured Alan could be at my house within 5 minutes after leaving work because the factory is just around the corner from where I live. If getting to spend time with Alan meant I'd lose a little sleep, I figured it was a small price to pay.

Sure enough, by 11:05 Alan walked through my front door. Before leaving my house during the wee hours of the morning, he asked if he could once again come over when he got off work that night. It only took a few nights before it became our routine for me to drive to work in Louisville, come home and nap a couple hours, then get up in time for Alan to come over when he got off work so we could spend some time together. It was always ALAN that showed up. Then, it only took a few more nights for him to stop leaving in the middle of the night and stay with me until I got up to go to work the next morning.

In late January, 2007, Alan moved in with me. Some of my family members made comments about us moving 'too fast,' but they weren't aware our relationship had been 15 years in the making. I was thoroughly enjoying masculine aggressive, sexually satisfying Alan. He even grew a beard. I saw no signs of 'Alana.' We continued our routine – me leaving for work in the morning – Alan leaving for work before I got home – me taking a nap for a couple hours then getting up in time to greet him at the door when he got off work at 11:00 p.m. We'd spend a few hours together and the intense energy we felt just from lying next to one another always turned into wonderfully satisfying sex. We'd finally fall asleep sometime between 2 or 3 a.m. Then the next morning I'd get up around 8:00 or 8:30 a.m., head back to Louisville, get home, take my nap, greet Alan at the door, and do it all over again.

The time we spent together between him getting home from work and us finally going to bed was usually spent with us lying on the couch with soft music playing and the lights low. One evening while I lay there in his arms he said, "Oh my God, I can't believe I'm holding Bobbie Thompson in my arms – living with Bobbie Thompson."

"Why did you say it that way?" I asked. "That you can't believe you're holding 'Bobbie Thompson' in your arms."

"This is a dream I've had all my life. I can't believe it's finally come true. Do you know I remember the first time I ever saw you."

"Do what?" I asked.

Then he repeated, "I remember the first time I ever saw you. It was at Glens Creek Baptist Church. I was around 15 years old. I was sitting on the right hand side in the second or maybe third pew from the front. Do you remember how the inside of the church was set up?"

"Yes, I remember. We usually sat on the right side too, about half-way back."

"I looked around to see if there were any other kids there my age. You were two or three rows behind me.

When I saw you I thought, 'wow, that's the most beautiful woman I've ever seen.' Because you were holding a baby and sitting next to a man, I figured you were married and turned away. But, I had to take just one more look and this time what caught my attention was the size of your huge breasts."

I laughed as I hit him jokingly and said, "Why am I not surprised that you were sitting in church lusting after my boobs."

"I've been attracted to you ever since that moment. Do you remember when my family moved into the house across the street from you on Elm Heights when I was around 19 years old?"

"Of course I remember."

"I used to bring my guitar out into the front yard to practice playing. I could have practiced anywhere, but I thought if I sat in the front yard maybe I'd get a chance to catch a glimpse of you across the street, even if you were doing nothing more than just walking to your car. Do you remember me playing my guitar in the front yard?"

"No, not really. Sorry. So, let me get this straight, you're telling me you've been pretty much stalking me for years? Is that right?"

"No. Not stalking. Just attracted to you. I never followed you around or anything creepy like that."

"Well, that's good to know. I was afraid I had a stalker on my hands." I laughed then continued, "The only thing I remember about you living across the street was when I broke my ankle while sleigh riding and how embarrassed I was because it was so difficult to get my fat ass back up the hill."

"I don't know why you were so embarrassed. It would have been difficult to get 'anyone' back up the hill with a broken ankle. Heavy or not makes no difference. Do you remember who took you to the hospital?"

"Of course I do. To this day I can't figure out how such a skinny kid about half my size picked me up and put me on that x-ray table."

We both laughed at that memory then Alan said, "That nurse asked me if I was your husband."

"Yeah, I know. I remember how red your face got when she asked you that and how quickly you lowered your head. I hated that she insulted you by asking if you were my husband."

"**INSULTED** me! Are you kidding? I was embarrassed because I was so happy that someone thought it **POSSIBLE** I could be your husband. As a matter of fact, when I finally went to my car to leave the hospital I just sat with my head down on my hands on the steering wheel basking in the thought of what it might be like to be your husband."

"As long as we've known each other you've never told me any of this before. You didn't even tell me any of this when we had our affair back in the day. Your secret attraction to me isn't the only thing you never got around to telling me about though, is it – you never told me about Alana either."

"No, for some reason I was never able to bring myself to discuss Alana with you. I've known since I was a kid I felt like a girl inside. The first time in my life I felt like I was dressed appropriately was when Ricky took a picture of me dressed in mom's clothes when I was 8 or 9 years old."

"You used to dress in your mom's clothes?"

"Just that once. Mom bought us a camera for Christmas and we were always taking pictures of the horses on the farm, pictures of the fences, trees, anything. I'd take pictures of Ricky, and Ricky would take pictures of me. But I never liked the way I looked in any of my pictures. One day I decided I wanted to look different and went into mom's room and put on one of her dresses, her wig, her shoes, and grabbed one of her purses before heading out for Ricky to take my picture. Everyone just thought I was playing one of my silly jokes, but it is the only picture I'd ever seen of me where I liked the way I looked. I think mom still has that picture actually. I'll see if she can find it and show it to you some time."

"Well, if you've known you were transgender since you were 8 years old, why didn't you tell someone – why didn't you tell me while we were having the affair?"

"At 8 I knew I was 'different,' but I didn't know anything about being transgender. Actually, that picture sent me into hiding – I felt ashamed of liking myself as a girl. I didn't understand *why* I felt the way I did, and I wasn't about to let anyone know how I felt. I was successful in hiding my feelings for years; I just wasn't able to keep them hidden. It was around the time that you and I were together I started learning there is such a thing as being transgender. The more I learned, the more I realized transgender explained the way I feel inside. I couldn't tell you anything about something I was just learning about myself."

Over the next couple days I tried to process in my mind all that Alan told me that night. I couldn't imagine a life of not understanding yourself, of having to hide who you are, of feeling ashamed of being 'you.' I was also trying to process what he told me about being attracted to me since he was 15 years old. He had never mentioned either of these things to me during the entire three years we'd shared a relationship. When I received his initial phone call that day wanting us to get together he had said, "Now I can tell you how attracted I've always been to you." I never realized he *literally* meant always.

Something else our conversation made me think about was my 'God' letters – where I write down the things I want in a letter to God then burn the letter – symbolic of the smoke delivering my letter to Heaven. I had written letters telling God what I wanted in a man and had gotten pretty much everything I'd asked for: a man younger than me, with thick lips, a good kisser, a big dick, wants sex, and has no interest in getting married. The last man I'd dated met everything I'd put in my letter. But, somehow that relationship seemed lacking. I knew I had no interest in marriage, but there had been no real connection – we enjoyed one another physically but were unable to carry on an intelligent conversation with one another.

Then I realized I had omitted something important from my God letter. I had omitted the man wanting not just sex, but wanting '*me*' or desiring '*ME*.' So, at the end of 2006, just a few weeks before Alan rang my doorbell, I wrote another letter to God, only this time, when I wrote the description of the man I wanted in my life I added 'he desires ME' in my letter. After what Alan had shared about being attracted to me since he was 15-years old, I couldn't imagine anyone else in the world desiring *me* more than he did. My God letter had yet again come to fruition as they often do.

One evening, while we were lying on the couch together, I asked, "If you feel like you should have been born a girl, how is it that you are such a good lover as a man?"

"Think about it," he said. "Who knows about what a woman likes more than a woman? I've often imagined, if I'd been born in a female body, what I would want a lover to do that would satisfy me sexually. I just do to you the things I've imagined I would enjoy having done to me." Then he kissed me softly, and I melted as always.

Another evening while we were lying on the couch together out of the blue he said, "I think the bitch is dead." I believed he could be right. He'd had his beard for a while and was nothing but masculine from my perspective. Secretly I really liked the idea of not having to deal with the whole transgender thing and would like to have been able to say, "Good, we don't have to worry with that freaky shit anymore." But instead, I felt sadness. Because I know Alan is such a kind, loving, caring, honest person hearing him call himself a bitch made my heart hurt. I said, "Don't say things like that because 'the bitch' is a part of you and I can't stand to think of any part of you as being dead."

Alan's work week ran from Sunday through Thursday so he'd still be at home when I'd get home from work on Friday. One Friday after a few weeks of living with bearded masculine aggressive Alan, I got home to find he had shaved off the beard. My thoughts were, *"I know what he's doing. He's fixing it so that 'Alana crap' can start up again. Well, I'm not going to put up with that shit. This isn't going to work –* **SHE** *might as well just move out right now."*

Alan must have been able to sense my thoughts because he dimmed the lights, turned the music on low, walked over to the couch, and motioned for me to come join him – our normal routine. I hesitated. Then he said, "I'm still me even without the beard."

I gave in and lay down beside him. I was gearing up to say, "I don't think this is going to work for me," but before I could say anything he hugged me tightly and said, "Honey, these are the same arms that have always held you, these are the same lips that have always kissed you, I still have the same level of education I've always had, and I can still change the tires on your car." Then he kissed me.

I never saw him/her as being the '*same*.' From my perspective there are two '*personalities*' – one male and one female. I'd enjoyed a lifelong friendship with the male – and had no interest in getting to know the female. Although I could 'sense' Alana because of a clean-shaven face I realized he was right – the arms still felt the same, the kiss still felt the same, and I still felt that intense sexual energy building inside me. It was at that moment I began to understand there isn't an 'Alan' and an 'Alana' but only ONE person, the same person – only one energy, the same energy – no matter what name used, or gender '*perceived.*' I never got around to saying, "I don't think this is working for me."

Alan had been living with me for several weeks when my son called to say he needed me to babysit my grandson, who had just turned four years old in December. I agreed, and then my son said, "Mom, we don't want him around Alan."

I asked, "Why?"

"Because of that weird transgender crap," he said. "I don't know anything about that stuff other than what we've heard, and you always hear that people like that are mental or child molesters."

"Alan is neither. Son, you've known Alan most of your life. You know the type of person he is. You know your child will be safe in Alan's company."

"I 'used to know' Alan," he said. "But I haven't been around him since I was a kid and I have no idea what might have gone on in his life to make him like he is now, and neither do you mom. You can't swear my child, or you, are safe with a person like that around."

"Son, you're just speaking out of fear of the unknown. You just said the only thing you know about someone being transgender is what you've heard from other people – people who don't have the experience of being transgender themselves so can only speculate what it's all about. So, like them, you're saying things and basing your fears on something you know nothing about. I'll tell you what let's do . . . let's all get together for dinner in a nice restaurant so you two can spend some time around Alan and we'll see where it goes."

"OK, we can do that," he said.

A couple nights later we met for dinner and my grandson immediately liked Alan. My son had known Alan since the time he was the age his son is now. He and Alan enjoyed a journey down memory lane so by the time dinner was over my son said, "OK, you can babysit your grandson." Then, within another couple weeks, my grandson was spending the night with us.

A few days later Alan told me he'd been contacted by Cassie, one of the friends Alana had made while attending the Transgender Support Group at the GLSO (Gay Lesbian Services Organization) in Lexington. Cassie had heard that Alana and Mary had separated and called to see how she was doing. She also invited Alana to attend the upcoming support group meeting scheduled for the following Saturday.

After their conversation Alan said to me, "It's been a long time since I've been to a support group meeting and would really like it if you would go with me. Of course, it will be Alana attending the meeting, and, you've never actually seen Alana." Then he hesitated and said, "Well, technically that's not true, you have actually seen Alana, because whenever anyone looks at me they're seeing Alana, *THEY* just don't realize it."

I thought for a minute before answering. I remembered how uncomfortable I'd been seeing Alana the day we'd gone to the mall together – and she wasn't even 'decked out.' But going to a support group meeting wouldn't be like actually being in public around 'normal' people. From what Alan had said about being the 'same arms, same lips, etc.' I knew Alan/Alana existed entwined within the same being so I decided since I knew she was there, I should at least get to know her by 'seeing' her. I'd seen a few pictures of Alana, but had never seen her in person. I thought this might be a good opportunity to help me decide how I felt about being around Alana. I figured if I was uncomfortable being in Alana's company going to a support group meeting, then we'd both know and the experience would help us break up easier if it came to that. Finally I said, "OK, I'll go with you. But, if I'm going to be seen in public with Alana, then we need to get Alana a wig – your thinning hair just isn't right for a girl."

Alana called Cassie to let her know we'd be attending the support group meeting and told her what I said about needing a wig. Cassie recommended Pamela Dee Wigs in Lexington and even volunteered to accompany us to the shop.

We met Pam and she was an absolute sweetheart. She has several clients who are transgender and, although all I saw was Alan, Pam called Alana by name. Pam would say things like, "have 'her' try this one on" or "I bet 'she' would look good in this style." It was a little awkward for me seeing a male and hearing female pronouns used – but I kept it to myself. I had never been around anyone referring to Alan as female before, and I could tell he liked it. Finally we found the perfect wig for Alana's slender face – it was a long straight style with bangs.

Saturday arrived and I helped Alan make the transformation into Alana. I did his make-up then watched as he put on a padded bra and slipped on a pair of pantyhose. I couldn't believe how good Alan's long legs looked with pantyhose on. I definitely got a sense of working with a female as Alan tried on first one outfit then another trying to decide what to wear. Once that decision was made came the final touches of choosing jewelry and putting on the wig.

I got the wig bobby-pinned in place on Alan's head, brushed it, and then stepped back as he stood up. Only I didn't see *him* anymore. There before me stood a tall thin woman. A beautiful woman. I could only say, "Holy shit – you're beautiful." **ALANA** grinned from ear to ear as I truly saw her for the first time.

I'd never been around anyone who is transgender. I'd attend drag shows, and it was very easy to see the drag queens as female. As a matter of fact, they were so female in my mind, that it was harder to imagine that they were actually men in drag. They were more female than a lot of females I know. That's the transformation Alan had just made right before my eyes, 'he' became 'she.'

We arrived at the Pride Center and I didn't really know what to expect. When we first walked into the room I felt a little uncomfortable. I was definitely outside my comfort zone being in a room full of transgender people ... an experience I'd never had before. What I saw was a mixing of two genders, something I knew nothing about and had no knowledge or understanding of. My only experiences had been when I initially saw Alana the first time in 2006 and then watching the transformation process from Alan to Alana just prior to coming to the meeting. I was comfortable with seeing Alana after watching the transformation process because my brain understood what I had witnessed. I understood how Alan became Alana. However, that first time I saw Alana even the word 'transgender' was unknown to me, and being faced with the unknown often brings fear ... actually, 'fear of the unknown' is the greatest fear we, as humans, ever face. It was 'fear of the unknown' that had caused me to initially react to Alana by telling her I thought she was a freak when I saw her for the first time. Upon entering the room and seeing the mixing of two genders – something unknown, or something I knew very little about -- again caused me to be uncomfortable.

I took a seat right next to Alana as the meeting began. I looked around the room as the transgender persons began discussing one matter then the next in relation to the meeting. It was like when I'd watched the drag shows. Because they were 'drag' shows, I was consciously aware that the 'women' in the shows were actually men, however, I quickly came to see them, or recognize them, only as women. And, because of what I'd come to understand about being transgender, I was consciously aware the transgender women had not been born genetic women, however, as I sat watching them ... taking in the way they talked ... their feminine mannerisms ... their feminine actions ... it didn't take long for my brain, and therefore my eyes, to start 'seeing' only women.

After a few minutes into the meeting one of the girls asked the question to everyone in attendance, "How do you explain when someone says to you they don't understand you."

Another girl responded, "I heard an explanation this week that I liked. Everyone recognizes a Coke bottle, even from a distance, because of its shape, right?"

Then the girl speaking hesitated for a second as if to let the question she had just asked about the Coke bottle sink in a bit. Everyone, including me, gave a slight nod as if we had all responded audibly with, "of course."

Then she continued, "What if when you open the Coke bottle you find there's Orange Crush inside? But because of the bottle's shape, you believed it was a Coke. What do you really have? Is it a Coke because of the packaging, or is it an Orange Crush because of what's inside?"

In my head I was thinking, *"WOW, that is a good explanation. It's always what's inside that counts."* I had gained an understanding that Alan/Alana is ONE from the earlier comments about the 'same arms, same lips,' etc. With the Coke bottle explanation I began understanding that, because Alana is a female '*on the inside*,' then she really is a female – no matter what I see on the outside. The Coke bottle example gave me a better understanding that the transgender women in the room are female. Having this information, this knowledge, this understanding helped me recognize transgender women as women. Prior to having this information I had no way of knowing anything about transgender women which had always caused confusion for me because of seeing a mixing of two genders ... now I had a different understanding ... a different definition for what I was seeing: "Transgender women are female, they just weren't biologically born into a female form."

After the meeting ended several people came over to chat with Alana who would, of course, introduce me. They were all really nice. One thing I noticed was how everyone was drawn to Alana. Alan has a very easy going personality and charismatic energy, but, Alana seemed even more at ease and her charismatic energy seemed heightened somehow. She just shined.

After a few minutes of chatting with everyone we got into our car and Alana asked, "So, what did you think?"

I answered, "I think they were all just people."

"So you were OK in there."

"Sure. I didn't really know what to expect at first, but, like I said, it was just a room full of people."

"Good. I'm glad you were OK with everything. Well, some of the girls are going to a gay bar and wanted to know if we'd like to join them there. I didn't know how you'd feel about going into a gay bar, so I told them I'd have to ask you first. It's called 'The Bar Complex.'

"I love the Bar Complex. They have the best dance floor in town," I answered excited over the prospect of getting to go dancing.

"You've been to The Bar Complex?" Alana asked in a surprised tone.

"Yes."

"When?"

"I used to work with a guy named Cary. He occasionally produces a benefit show at the Bar Complex. His performer name is Jennifer. I attended one of his shows."

"Cool, so we can go then?"

"Sure. Sounds like fun to me."

Alana and I joined some of her friends at the bar where I got to chat more with Cassie, Kallie, and Samantha. I instantly loved each one of them. We had so much fun that night. Because her friends hadn't seen Alana for quite some time, first one then another would buy her a drink. She was very drunk by the time we left – but that didn't matter because I knew she was happy – extremely happy. The feeling I got from seeing the person I love being so happy is undescribable.

****

A couple weeks after going to the transgender support group meeting Alan came to me and said, "Honey, I haven't been to talk to my therapist, Marcie Hill, for a couple years now. I think the last appointment I had with her was just before I took that over-the-road truck driving job. I've talked to her on the phone a time or two since then, but haven't actually had an appointment. So many things have changed that I think I'd like to go see her again."

"Sounds good to me. I know how much going to Dr. Stith helped me. I see no problem whatsoever with talking to a therapist – in fact, I'd highly recommend it for anyone."

"I was kinda hoping you'd go with me," he said.

"OK. I've heard you talk quite a bit about Marcie so I'd like to meet her anyway. Just make an appointment and let me know when we need to go."

"It's next Tuesday at 2:30," he smiled.

We arrived at Marcie's office and she was as Alan had described, absolutely beautiful inside and out. We were lead into the session room and as we sat down she said, "Bobbie, it's nice to finally get to meet you. I feel like I know you already because of things Alana has shared with me about your history together."

I felt my face flush as I smiled and lowered my head not really knowing what to say. She smiled too then turned to Alan and said, "Well, Alana, it's been a long time since we've seen one another. I heard you and Mary had divorced. I'm sorry."

"We decided it would be best to divorce as friends than to try to make things work then wind up hating one another. Bobbie and I are living together now."

"Congratulations," she said.

Then Alan continued, "She went to a Support Group Meeting with me. Something I could never convenience Mary to do."

Marcie then looked at me and said, "How did that go?"

I responded, "I was fine with it. It didn't take me but a minute to figure out that people are just people.

Actually, I learned a couple things I never would have known if I hadn't gone to that meeting with Alan, uh, Alana. I'm sorry. I still have difficulty with the names and pronouns."

"That's understandable. Especially when you're dealing with someone you've known as long as you two have known one another. What did you learn?"

"Well, the first thing I learned is that I'm a GG – a 'genetic girl.' No one had ever called me a GG prior to attending the meeting with …" I let my sentence end there not really knowing which name I should use.

Marcie caught what I had done and just smiled as she asked, "And what else did you learn?"

"Well, there was a man there that I knew. We'd worked together and had even attended the same social function once. He looked scared to death when he saw me come into the meeting. After the meeting was over he asked me to step outside to talk. He said he wanted to make sure I kept his 'secret.' I told him I wasn't the type of person to share people's secrets and if he wanted to be a woman then that was his business and no one else's. That's when he spoke up and said, "Do what? No, I don't 'want' to be a woman, I'm transgender. I was BORN a female. I transitioned and moved here to get a job where no one would know my past." Then it was my turn to say, "Do what?" I had no idea. By the time we left I believe he felt comfortable that his secret was safe with me."

She laughed as she said, "I think people would be surprised at the number of transgender individuals there are in the area. Like you, many of the people they know and work with have no idea they are transgender."

"Well, I certainly had no idea this man was transgender."

Marcie then turned her attention back to Alana and said, "You've had a lot going on since our last session."

"I sure have," Alana said, "the biggie of course is getting with Bobbie. You know I've talked about her to you in many of my sessions, I just never thought she'd ever actually be here with me."

The rest of the session was spent with Alana getting Marcie caught up with what all had happened and what was going on now. By the time the session was over I felt more like we'd visited an old friend than had a therapy session. Our time together had been so enjoyable that when she asked if we wanted to make another appointment I was eager to say 'yes.'

07

BECOMING ACQUAINTED WITH ALANA

For the first several months of us living together my routine of spending the weekends going out dancing with my girlfriends didn't slow down much – we just included Alan. Of course, both Vallarie and Chiquita were somewhat familiar with him because I had told them about 'the man I'd had an affair with back in the day' so they already knew how I felt about him as a lover. They really liked Alan, but simply couldn't imagine and had never seen Alana. They had difficulty comprehending how this tall, masculine, blue-jean wearing, long haired, leather jacketed, sexy 'man' could possibly feel like he was a woman. That's when I'd share the Coke bottle example I'd heard in the support group meeting – and they also agreed that it's what's inside that counts. Then I'd say, "Well, just like seeing the Coke bottle and not being aware there is Orange Crush inside, it's easy to see Alan and never know Alana is there on the inside."

Once I was asked, "How do you think you'd feel if he decided to cheat on you with a man some day?"

"I'd probably feel about the same as when I learned Little Redneck had been cheating on me. Who someone cheats with is of no concern because there's no connection between myself and that person. I could care less about that person ... so it doesn't matter if that person is a male or female ... what matters is the damage done by the loss of trust between me and the person I'm in a relationship with ... it's the dishonesty that causes the hurt."

But, they'd still say, "I just don't see how you handle being in a relationship with a man who wants to be a woman. I'm not sure I could do that. But, if you're happy, then that's all that matters to us."

After a while Alan and I grew tired of partying every weekend and soon began going out with my friends less and less. We began spending more and more time at home and fell into the habit of reading books. Alan would sit at one end of the couch with his back against the arm listening, and I would sit at the other end reading. One of the first books we read together was *"Ask and it is Given: Learning to Manifest Your Desires,"* one of the 'Abraham' books by Esther and Jerry Hicks. Like me, Alan had been raised in a Baptist church and had never been exposed to the idea that we are 'spiritual beings having a physical experience.'

It turned out that reading the Abraham books was a great starting point for building the foundation of our relationship. As I'd read, what I was reading would trigger a thought in my mind. Often I'd stop reading and say, "This passage makes me think of . . ." then share whatever thoughts had crossed my mind.

Alan, in his slow, soft, easy-going manner, would think for a second or two as he rubbed his chin before speaking, "Really? I would never have thought of it like that," he'd say calmly, then continue with, "what that passage brings to my mind is . . ." and he'd share whatever meaning the passage had for him and usually it was something totally the opposite from what it had meant to me.

Reading and sharing our thoughts with one another turned out to be a valuable lesson for me. I realized if it had been Alan reading the passage and he had been the first to speak and say to me, "This passage makes me think of . . ." I most likely would have snapped a response, without even thinking, as I sometimes do, with something like, "That's the craziest bullshit I've ever heard." But, as it turned out, a very valuable lesson I learned was how extremely different our thinking processes are – we don't think alike in any way, shape, form, or fashion. Because of Alan's slow gentle response, we were able to discuss our different views rather than argue about them and share with one another the basis for our point of view. Hearing one another's explanations gave each other a different perspective, but there are still many many things we don't agree on – but we learned to allow each other to have our own opinions based on our own perspective without either being 'right' or 'wrong.' Reading together helped us learn, and practice the skill of communication early in our relationship.

Not long after this lesson learned I read a comment that said, "IF we were able to get inside one another's head and see how differently we each think, we'd swear we were all from a different planet because no two people think alike." After my experiences with examples of how my and Alan's thinking processes are so very different, I believed that statement could be true.

****

By mid-May 2007 I'd had enough of driving 60 miles one way from Versailles to Louisville then back at the end of a long work day. I enjoyed being a mortgage loan originator, and learned quite a bit about the industry, but I hated all that driving, so I moved my license to an office in Lexington working much closer to home. Not long after my move, Alan got moved to day shift at the factory and our lives were beginning to take on a normal routine. We'd be home together in the evenings and I no longer had to take naps in order to be able to greet him at the door when he got off work.

October was fast approaching and for the last several years Vallarie, Chiquita, and I had gone to the big Halloween bash at Jim Porter's Good Time Emporium in Louisville. Chiquita decided she wouldn't be able to attend this year, so Alan and I decided to go with Vallarie – only it would be Alana present at the Halloween party since we'd decided to go as Sonny and Cher. A couple of friends, Joe and Heather, decided to attend the Halloween party with us. They knew me and Vallarie, had met Alan, and was aware of, but had never seen Alana.

Not long after arriving at the hotel where we would all stay, we began the process of transforming Alan into Alana, or rather into Cher on this occasion. Alana showered and put on her bra, pantyhose, and robe and I had just started applying her makeup by covering her face in concealer. Right at that moment there was a knock at the door. I continued putting on the layer of concealer as I asked, "Who is it."

The response came, "It's me, Vallarie, and I'm already in my costume so I decided to visit with you guys while you get ready."

"Give me a second," I said, "I'll be right there."

All of a sudden Alana's breathing pattern became strained – it was as if she had suddenly been frightened. Before going to the door I asked her, "What's the matter?"

She blew out a couple quick breaths and said, "I know you've told your friends about Alana, but knowing about Alana and seeing Alana for the first time are two different things. I don't know if they can handle this – I don't know if *'I'* can handle this."

"Don't be silly," I said, "after all, we are talking about MY friends and if they weren't open minded and a little on the weird side themselves, they probably wouldn't be MY friends."

I think if she could have Alana would have stopped me from going to the door. As I swung the door open Vallarie bolted into the room and said, "Are you guys about ready."

"No, not yet, I'm applying Alana's makeup," I said as Vallarie walked right past me and toward the bathroom where Alana was as I closed the door behind her.

Without skipping a beat she said, "That foundation is way to light for him, I mean her."

"That's not the foundation," I said as I returned to the bathroom, "I've just started putting on the concealer."

"Well, you go start getting ready and I'll do his makeup, I mean her makeup." She then shook her head as if trying to get it all straightened out in there. She laughed and said, "This is kinda confusing, isn't it."

But without saying anything else she picked up Alana's foundation and continued with the makeover. I smiled as I looked at Alana and could tell her anxiety had disappeared. Without realizing what she had done, Vallarie had instantly put Alana at ease.

Right as we were putting on the finishing touches of our costumes the phone in the room rang – it was Joe and Heather, "Are you guys about ready yet?"

"Yes, we're getting ready to head out the door," I said.

"We tried calling Vallarie, but she didn't answer her phone. Do you know if she's already downstairs?"

"No, she's here with us. Do you guys want to meet us here in the room or just meet us in the lobby?"

"We'll just meet you in the lobby. We're heading there now."

"OK, we'll see you in a few."

The next hurdle was to get Cher to step out of the room and walk down the hall to the elevator. Luckily Sonny (me), Cher (Alana) and a female Pirate (Vallarie) were the only people in the elevator. As it came to a stop on the Lobby Level we stepped out and Joe and Heather (a Neanderthal couple) greeted us. Joe walked up to Alana and said, "Well hello Cher," as he extended an elbow for Cher to take hold, "I've always wanted to take Cher out." We all stepped around the corner into the hotel lobby and were greeted with quite a site – a lobby full of all sorts of various costumes and creatures. All of a sudden, Alana no longer felt 'out of place.'

****

Alana and I had been living together for several months by the time Thanksgiving rolled around. It had been our practice for my sister Mitzi and I to host our family's holiday gatherings, usually by doing Thanksgiving at one house, then Christmas at the other. Mitzi called me in order for us to figure out who was doing what this year. She said she wasn't sure how she'd feel about knowing Alan wants to be a girl and coming to her house – and was sure her husband would have a difficult time with the situation. I told her pretty much the same thing I'd said to my son when he voiced opposition about being around Alan. I said, "Mitzi, Alan is still the same person he's always been. You liked him, and ran around with him back in the day when you weren't aware he was transgender. And it's not like he just all of a sudden became transgender. Even back then when you two were running around together HE was aware of who he is and has always been that same person. He won't be wearing a dress to your house for dinner. He's the same person you've always known and will look exactly like you've always seen him."

Thanksgiving Day arrived and we showed up at her house. Mitzi and Alan share a history together of being friends from back in the day, and another thing they share is smoking. When Mitzi was ready to go outside to smoke, Alan followed. It didn't take Mitzi long to feel comfortable talking with her old friend again. She still had no understanding of why 'he' would want to be a 'she,' but reconnecting with an old friend turned out just fine.

****

A friend invited me to attend a "Premier Jewelry" home party. I went and had such a good time with the girls – trying on all the pretty jewelry – acting all girly. Then the thought came to me, *"I know who would really enjoy a party like this – Alana – she's more 'girly' than I ever thought about being."* That's when the light bulb in my mind came on, *"Why not host a Premier Jewelry party and invite some of the T-girls I've gotten to know from attending the monthly Support Group meetings with Alana."*

As soon as I got the opportunity I pulled the Premier Jewelry Representative, Lynn, aside and said, "I think I'd like to book a party, but some of the girls I'd like to invite were born in a male body. Would you be comfortable doing a party with transgender women in attendance?"

She instantly said, "I don't care who comes to the party as long as they're interested in buying jewelry."

"Believe me; these girls will be interested in jewelry."

We set the date of May 18, 2008 for my Premiere Jewelry party and as Lynn handed me the invitations to send out she said, "Be sure to ask your guests to bring some of their favorite outfits and I can show them how to accessorize with some of the jewelry pieces."

The day of the party arrived and there were 4-transgender women, 3-genetic women, and one gay man in attendance. When Lynn first began her presentation I could tell she was a little nervous, but, as the ladies oohed and aahed over the pieces she was showing, she quickly became comfortable and within minutes she was calling the ladies, 'honey' and treating them just like she had treated the genetic women who had attended the party my friend had invited me to.

After Lynn showed the newest pieces of the season she said, "Now, who brought outfits so we can really have some fun with accessorizing?" Every one of the transwomen raised their hands.

First one then another would go into our spare bedroom to slip into what she had brought and then come back into the living room where Lynn would spruce up the outfit with various pieces of jewelry. More oohing and aahing followed as each of the ladies modeled their accessorized outfits. We were all enjoying how adding a broach here or a particular necklace made the outfit look so much more stylish.

It was quite a successful, and enjoyable, party. Lynn made quite a bit of money that afternoon, and I got a lot of free Premiere Jewelry. I think the gay man's was the largest purchase. The party was such fun for everyone.

Not all the trans-women in attendance get to live in female mode full time, so since they were all prettied up, we decided to go out to a restaurant together after the party ended – and the gay man joined us.

We decided which restaurant to meet at and each got into our respective cars to head to Lexington. When we arrived at the restaurant's parking lot everyone started to get out of their cars and I opened my car door. Alana grabbed my arm and said, "Wait a minute."

I looked at her and asked, "Why?"

"I'm not sure I can do this," she said.

"What do you mean you're not sure you can do this? I don't understand."

"I'm not sure I can get out of this car dressed like this."

"I still don't understand. You're always dressed like this when we go to the Support Group meetings."

"Yeah, it's easier when I know I'm going someplace

where I'm accepted. I have no problem going to the Support Group meetings dressed, but even going there dressed the first couple times was difficult. I'm not sure I can go into a family oriented restaurant dressed like this. I've always had a fear of some kid asking their parent why that man's wearing a dress – then the poor parent having to explain something they were wondering about themselves."

"Honey, you're not the only transwoman here. Look, everyone else is already out of their cars and waiting for you. Come on. We're here. I'm here. It will be OK."

With that she took a long deep breath, blew out hard, and opened her car door.

I could tell the way she was walking slightly behind my left shoulder with her head tilted down she was still uncomfortable. I immediately felt like I needed to take on an 'I'm your protector' role as I positioned myself between Alana and everyone else as we walked into the restaurant and to our table.

I kept my eye out to see what the reaction might be from the restaurant's patrons, but no one was paying any attention to our table. It hadn't dawned on me that Alana had never been 'out' in public, except for attending the Support Group meetings and occasionally going to gay bars. *"Humph,"* I thought, *"I never before realized how difficult it could be for someone to simply walk into a restaurant."*

The fun that began at the jewelry party continued through the meal with everyone laughing, telling jokes, and enjoying one another's company. It didn't take long for even Alana to begin feeling comfortable and enjoying herself – out – in public – in a family oriented restaurant.

The months seemed to fly by with Alan working days and me working as a mortgage loan originator. When we'd get home in the evening we continued to spend most of our time together lying on the couch – either with me reading or us just lying in one another's arms talking. We had enjoyed reading Esther Hick's, "Ask and it is Given" so much, we read several other 'Abraham' books she'd written. We also enjoyed James Redfield's *"Celestine Prophecy,"* and several books in his Celestine series, as well as Dan Brown's, *"Angels and Demons"* and *"The DaVinci Code."*

We also enjoyed watching movies along the same lines as the books we read – movies like *"The Secret," "What the Bleep Do We Know,"* and *"You Can Heal Your Life"* – all geared toward positive thinking. I continued to share with everyone that I attribute my life going from 'woe is me' to 'I love my life' to the power of positive thinking, and believe the statement is absolutely true that says, "Change your thoughts, change your life."

Mary Cynthia had introduced me to positive thinking when she invited me to her 'woo woo' workshop, and since that time I'd been living life based on what I'd learned, and continue to learn. Alan and I had been living together for just over a year and a half and, of course, with the books we were reading and the movies we were watching, he began to experience some changes as well. The greatest change experienced was when his doctors, all three of them, said, "I have no idea what you're doing, but keep up the good work. If you hadn't already been diagnosed with HIV, and you can't be undiagnosed, but, if we hadn't already, we would be unable to diagnose you with HIV today through a simple blood test. The virus is undetectable."

We did some research and learned that by taking the prescribed HIV medications as directed, an undetectable status is very possible to achieve. However, I believe maintaining a positive attitude also played a big part in achieving the undetectable status. I believe, just like the doctor on the movie "The Secret" states, 'Incurable' means 'curable from within.'

****

I'd known Alan for nearly 30-years, but it's true you never really know someone until you live with them – and even when you **think** you know everything about someone, you could be wrong. Alan and I had enjoyed our sexual relationship back in the day, but we hadn't spent much of our time talking whenever we had the opportunity to be together back then.

The entire time we'd been living together, except on those rare occasions when we'd go to the support group meetings, it was Alan I *saw*. I'd occasionally get a glimpse of Alana through a gesture or comment, but rarely *saw* her. I'd worked late one evening and on the way home I called and gave Alan instructions on getting supper started. When I got home the site I found in the kitchen stopped me dead in my tracks. Alan, or rather, Alana stood at the stove cooking while dressed in a black leather mini-skirt and wearing six-inch heels. Although I'd seen Alana on those occasions when we attended the support group meetings, it had always been easy for me because I had been a part of the transformation process of me seeing Alan become Alana. Those times I had witnessed the transformation into Alana were few and had happened on 'special' occasions.

But this wasn't a special occasion. This was just every-day living. Somehow, me helping Alan transform into Alana on those special occasions was OK, but walking in and finding my *'man'* dressed like a *'woman,'* at home, with no intention of going out, for no particular reason, just wasn't right – it wasn't *'NORMAL.'* It just wasn't something I was used to seeing – hell; I'd never seen it before actually – not in our daily home life setting.

As I stepped into the kitchen, Alana lowered her head slightly as she looked my direction, and in a very feminine manner said, "I figured if you were going to make me take on the role of 'woman of the house,' I'd dress the part too."

At first my mind was a total blank while reeling from the shock of walking in to witness a sight that was so foreign to me. Immediately I began asking myself questions and answering myself in my mind as I thought, *"I guess I don't have to be present for the process of transforming into Alana. If you're 'transgender,' then you're ALWAYS TRANSGENDER and not just on those 'special' occasions"* Then for further clarification and rationalization to help me deal with this my thoughts continued, *"So, dressing like this on a daily basis could be 'normal' behavior for a transgender person. Holy shit, did I just say 'normal' to myself about this site in front of me when I find it to be so 'abnormal?'* I guess I did, and what a revelation actually – this is NORMAL for some people, for transgender people. Wow – can I handle knowing I could walk in and encounter this sight, without warning, at any given moment in time? Damn good question and I'm not sure my answer is "yes." It is a bit of a shock to my system. But, then again, if someone had said to me at the Mall that first time I saw Alana, 'you're going to be living with Alana within a month,' I would have said, 'Bull Effin Shit,' but here we are."

My moment of self-talk helped me recover from the initial shock and I finally spoke, "Well, honey, I got news for you. I don't know any 'woman of the house' who wears a leather mini-skirt and six-inch heels, unless they're a 'woman' of a 'house of ill repute.'"

She then turned to me, grabbed my hand, ran it under her mini-skirt, said, "Play your cards right and it could be," and then kissed me.

She wasn't wearing any underwear. *"Hum,"* I thought, *"Alan was telling the truth that day when he was lying on the couch and said it was the 'same lips' as always. That was the same kiss I'd gotten from Alan so many times."* Alana kissed me again and within a matter of minutes I felt a penis hardening in my hands. My own sexual energy began to rise and more kisses followed. Then I thought, *"Yep, it's the same everything all right – same person, same kisses, same intense sexual energy. And, these clothes sure makes for easy access, this might not be such a bad thing after all. Oh well, we can live only one day at a time, and this day just might turn out to be a pretty good one after all."* I smiled, she smiled, and it didn't matter to me what she was wearing any more.

Over time, although it didn't happen on a daily basis, there were days I'd come home to find Alan in female attire, and as hard as I tried to be OK with it, those occasions just didn't sit well with me. There was always a moment of initial shock before I could adjust to what I was seeing. I was at least beginning to have some understanding of the concept of transgender, so I was confused as to why I was having such an adverse reaction to seeing Alan wearing a dress.

Then it dawned on me, I was uncomfortable with what I saw, **BECAUSE** I *'saw Alan'* in *'female'* clothing. I *saw* a male trying to look like a female. On those occasions when I had been involved in the transformation process my brain easily recognized the changing from male form to female form. However, by not being witness to the transformation, I saw a mixing of genders and that caused me confusion ... initial shock. I believe the shock came from having no words for understanding seeing a mixture of two genders – no way to mentally process within my own mind seeing a mixing of two genders.

When trying to understand the process of transitioning from one form to another, – or from one gender to another – I always think of the transformation process of the caterpillar-cocoon-butterfly. When we see a caterpillar we know what it is because it has a name, a word we use that gives us understanding of what we're looking at – caterpillar. Same thing when we see a male – we use the word man. When we see a butterfly we know what it is because it has a name, a word we use that gives us understanding of what we're looking at – butterfly. Same thing when we see a female – we use the word woman. When we see a cocoon we know what it is because it has a name, a word we use that gives us understanding of what we're looking at – we use the word cocoon to understand the transformation process from caterpillar to butterfly. When we see a cocoon we see neither the caterpillar nor the butterfly, nor do we see a 'mixture' of caterpillar and butterfly. What we see is a 'cocoon' – it has its own identifier, its own name. Cocoon is what we call the stage of *being* where the transformation takes place from caterpillar to butterfly. All very easily understood and accepted within our own mind.

When I see Alan in female clothing, my mind makes an attempt to 'identify' what I'm seeing in order to give *ME* understanding. But, I have no name to give that stage of the mixing of two genders – no words such as 'cocoon' to understand what I'm seeing.

I am just fine when I see Alan – like seeing the caterpillar. I am just fine when I see Alana – like seeing the butterfly. But when Alan/Alana is in a stage of being where I see a mixing of two genders – where I see a confusion of both male and female – I'm uncomfortable and believe that uncomfortable feeling comes from having no words, no name of identification, to give my brain understanding of what I'm seeing. I know no words used for the cocoon stage for human transitioning from one gender to the other; therefore, I am confused and made uncomfortable because of my own inability to understand what I see when I see Alan in women's clothing – in the process of transition.

When I witness the process of Alan becoming Alana through the application of makeup, a wig, and female clothing, I'm not uncomfortable because through witnessing the process, my mind can follow and understand. But, when I see a mixture of the two genders, without having witnessed the transforming process, it causes confusion in my own mind because I am unable to readily identify, or therefore choose which pronoun or name is appropriate for me to use. I am very much aware that when I look at this person, whether I use the pronoun 'he' or 'she' and whether I use the name 'Alan' or 'Alana' I am viewing one individual which encompasses the entirety of he, she, Alan, Alana. It is within *'me,'* it is my own perspective that determines which pronoun and/or name I use.

I've learned to choose my 'seeing', choose the pronouns, and say either Alan or Alana based on the gender being presented which is usually defined by the attire being worn at that moment. It's not uncommon for me to identify Alan as he sits on the riding lawn mower and does yard work. Then when he comes in hot and sweaty from doing the yard work he gets into the shower. After showering, Alana likes to wear a particular simple little purple summer dress around the house for its comfort and coolness. Prior to the shower I 'see' Alan. After the shower, I 'see' Alana. But, both before the shower, and after the shower, I'm 'seeing' the same person. I just see that person differently and can only speak from MY perspective. No one 'sees' a caterpillar and 'says' butterfly.

****

In addition to watching movies we call positive thinking movies, we also began watching movies that would help me learn more about transgender people. I'd watched only one such movie before – the 1992 release of *"The Crying Game."* It had been several years back even before I was aware of Alana's existence.

I'd been flipping the TV channels when I came across

a movie that was just beginning and decided to watch it because it starred Forest Whitaker, and I like him as an actor, so I left the TV on that station. I had no clue as to the 'surprise' and when it was revealed in the movie, just like the character's reaction (he threw up) it made me feel like I wanted to throw up too. It was kinda like the train wreck situation where I was too engrossed to look away, so, I kept watching, and by the end I felt differently about the transwoman in the movie.

My change of heart over *"The Crying Game"* reminded me of watching *"Harry and the Henderson's"* with John Lithgow (another one of my favorite actors) when my daughter was around 5-years old. When that movie first began she climbed up behind my left shoulder and buried her head in my neck frightened as she said, "Mommy, you brought home the wrong movie, this is scary." I sat her in my lap and assured her she was safe with mommy. I told her we'd have to watch the movie to learn more about Harry before we could know for sure whether or not he was scary. Sure enough, at the end of the movie when Harry is released back into the woods she again buried her head in my neck, but this time she was crying as she said, "I don't want Harry to go. I like Harry." She, like I had done with *"The Crying Game,"* had a complete change of heart after learning the truth vs believing the first impression. Decisions are so much better made AFTER you have all the information.

The first trans movie Alan and I watched together is one called, *"Normal"* with Tom Wilkinson and Jessica Lang that was made in 2003. I recognized things in that movie that I'd experienced with Alan – including feeling uncomfortable seeing 'him' (Tom Wilkinson) trying to be 'her' and my mind still identifying 'him' as 'him.' We humans tend to become uncomfortable whenever we're faced with anything that is outside of our own experiences – outside of what is normal for us – and watching the movie *"Normal"* was uncomfortable for me, but it gave me a point of understanding I would not otherwise have had.

The next such movie we watched was a documentary called, *"Beautiful Daughters."* It was the first movie about transwomen where I truly **SAW** women – where my mind didn't try to identify what I was looking at as a man trying to be a woman – these women were truly women – full-fledged butterflies. Although all the women taught me something by sharing their experience of being a transwoman, (and every person's experience is different from any other person's experience) there were three who stood out for me, Leslie Townsend, Lynn Conway, and Valerie Spencer – but it was what Valerie Spencer said that absolutely made my spirit jump because it was her words that gave me a perspective, an understanding, that had never crossed my mind before but helped me have a better acceptance of Alana. She said, "Some women have penises, I'm one of them and I don't ever want to get rid of it ... I'm to keep mine AND embrace my womanhood ... I'm not trapped in a penis' body."

"WOW," I thought. There in front of me was a vibrant, radiant, beautiful **WOMAN** telling me, and the world, that she, this particular woman, had been born with a penis and she said 'some women,' are born with a penis, which meant there were other women in the world who have a penis too. It took me a minute or two to wrap my brain around such a concept, but she proclaimed it to

be true – and I believed her. For the first time I understood that some women have a penis. It was those words that helped me understand that Alana is a WOMAN who has a penis. Previously the only way I could understand Alana's experience was that of a man wanting to be a woman which is a totally different concept than the understanding Alana IS A WOMAN born with a penis.

****

By the end of September 2008 I'd had enough of the mortgage loan industry – or, rather, I'd had enough of the 'lack of business' and no income from the mortgage loan industry. Apparently, I'd chosen the absolute worst time in history to become a mortgage loan originator and was just glad I at least had a retirement income. One day while sitting bored in my mortgage loan office I simply made the decision to give it up.

My first on the side endeavor to bring additional income into the household was in the late 1970's – I was a Tupperware lady. I continued the practice of 'sales' in one form or another as a sideline and had given up my latest venture in 2006 – when I had been a Passion Parties representative (or, as my son called me, I was a 'dildo dealer'). I decided to check out several sales positions with some MLM companies and before long I had joined a few I liked. I wasn't making any money as a mortgage loan originator, and figured a multi-level marketing business, or two, had the possibility of helping me earn more than nothing.

Alan would get up and go to the factory, and I'd spend my day doing house work, setting up sales presentations, and checking out various other income ventures that interested me. One day in mid-December I heard Alan coming in the back door and immediately knew something was wrong because he'd left the house to go to work just a little over an hour ago. "What's wrong?" I asked as he walked in.

"Well, honey, I just lost my job," was his answer.

"Yeah, right," I said.

"I'm serious. A guard stopped me as I walked toward the factory door and said, 'You need to report to the office.' I had no idea why I needed to go to the office, but it didn't take long to figure it out when I found ten other guys in the office too." He then laid a file-folder down and said, "Here's what they gave me."

"Oh shit," I thought. *"This can't be good,"* as I instantly got a sinking feeling and my stomach became one huge knot. Then I remembered what I'd learned from the various books we'd read and from watching *"The Secret."* The way you 'feel' is your body's 'emotional guidance system,' – in other words, the way you 'feel' is your body communicating with you. When you feel 'good,' your attention or focus is going in the right direction. When you feel 'bad,' your attention or focus is going in the wrong direction.

At that moment I was feeling really really bad. So I thought, *"Losing your job is a bad thing. How can I NOT feel bad over something as devastating as this?"* Then again, like had happened to me before, it was as if a voice in my head said, *"It is what it is and you can't change the fact that Alan no longer has a job but you can choose how you're going to react to that fact. You have two choices. You can let it devastate you, stop you in your tracks, and feel bad about it, or, you can take a look at it from a different perspective and figure out what steps you need to take to go forward from this point."*

"Oh well, it is what it is." I said, " and from my perspective we have two choices – choose to fall apart and become devastated, or choose to practice what we preach which is to 'let go and let God.' Personally, I think the second option is our best choice. Sometimes when things happen to us that we classify as a bad thing, it can turn out to be a blessing in disguise. Who knows, maybe that's what this will turn out to be. I know you weren't happy with that job anyway, and I know you wouldn't have given it up because you had such a difficult time finding a job when you finally got that one. To me, this could just be God closing one door to force us to turn our attention to a door He's going to open for us. Now, let's take a look at what's important here and what options we have available to us. Of course, I guess health insurance is our biggest concern. Where do you stand insurance wise?"

Alan pointed to the folder he'd laid down and said, "That's one of the things we discussed in the office this morning. My current insurance will lapse in 30 days, so, I have insurance until mid-January. After that, COBRA will go into effect. But, of course, there's a high cost to COBRA."

We opened the folder to take a look at the cost of COBRA and all of a sudden I felt that sinking feeling again. "Damn, that's expensive," I said.

"Not only is it expensive, but COBRA only lasts for so long – which means I have to find another job before that time runs out."

"Thank God I don't have to worry about insurance. My health insurance is very low cost because I'm retired from state government. Of course, it's just an individual policy. Family coverage costs more. I bet COBRA costs more per month than what a family policy would cost a retired state employee." That's when the idea hit me so I continued, "You know . . . if we got married you could go on my insurance and you'd have it for the rest of your life so you'd never have to worry again about not having insurance. It would eliminate the stress of being in a hurry to find another job too. You'd probably be able to find a better job if you didn't feel like you just had to accept the first thing that came along just for the benefits."

"Wait a minute. Did you just say get married?"

"Well, it's not like we haven't discussed marriage, we'd just be doing it a little sooner than we expected."

I made a phone call to check on the cost of coverage for a family plan insurance policy should we decided to get married. Turns out I was right – COBRA was the more expensive of the two choices. I put the phone down and turned to Alan, "Well, it looks like getting married earlier versus later might be a viable choice for us. BUT, we need to talk about something first. I love you but I never want to change my last name again. My children are Thompsons, my grandson is a Thompson, and I want to keep my name just the way it is."

"That's fine with me. If anyone asks why we have different last names I'll just tell them it's because you haven't proven yourself worthy to have the Sholar name."

We both laughed, but then he got a serious look on his face as he said, "There's so much more for us to consider here than just whether or not you're going to change your last name. How do you feel about being married to a woman some day?"

"I'm not really sure how I feel about that at this point in time. However, two years ago on that December day in 2006 when we went to the Mall together if someone had said, 'How do you feel about falling in love with and living with Alana?' I'd probably screamed 'HELL NO,' but that's exactly what's happened. At this moment I have no idea how I'll feel when you're transition is complete. That's one of those 'we'll cross that bridge when we get to it' things. But I can tell you this – because I know how far we've come since that December day I believe everything will be just fine."

He reached out and hugged me tightly and said, "I've come to learn that you can take any negative situation and work right through it until it's something positive, but, believe me, when I walked into this house with the news I'd just lost my job, I never dreamed I'd be this happy within a matter of a couple hours."

The next step was to set a wedding date. We knew we'd have to be married within 30 days so the new insurance would take effect before the old insurance ran out. I called my friend Vallarie because she ran a small catering business on the side and I knew she could help. Since I'd made little to no income through the mortgage industry the last couple years our budget was already pretty tight. Now, with the loss of Alan's income, we knew it would get even tighter, so we didn't have a lot of money to spend on the wedding.

First Vallarie and I tried to figure out the venue. Of course, that would depend on how many people we invited. If we invited only family – our parents, our children, our brothers and sisters with their children – we figured that would be 25 people – and that was just our families – we had friends to take into consideration as well. Then we talked about what to feed people if we're going to cater the wedding. Of course, there's the wedding cake, but you can't just let them eat cake.

I couldn't get anything worked out. For nearly two weeks I figured, I fretted, I planned, and I was running out of time. Finally, on Monday, December 29, 2008 I was frustrated with trying to figure it all out and said to Alan, "You know if we can pull off getting married before midnight on Wednesday, December 31st we'll be able to file our taxes together this year and get back a bigger income tax refund. We could use the refund to help pay off some bills since we're not sure where we'll be financially for a while."

He looked in my direction with a rather blank look on his face. Neither spoke as we both just kinda smiled at one another, jumped up, ran to the car, and headed to the courthouse to get our marriage license.

Two days later, Wednesday, December 31, 2008 at 1:30 p.m. we stood in our own living room with Indian Spirit music playing softly on the stereo, the Reverend Arthur Ulmer (my step-father) officiating the ceremony, with Raymond and Lois Sholar (Alan's parents) as our witnesses and 'Alana Nicole Sholar' and I were married saying the following vows which we had written ourselves:

PREACHER: *Loved ones, we come together today to join this couple in holy matrimony as they stand before you, one another, and God to pledge their love and their desire to become as one.*

In the presence of God and those gathered do you, Bobbie, take Alana to be your lifelong partner?
BOBBIE: *I do.*
PREACHER: *In the presence of God and those gathered do you, Alana, take Bobbie to be your lifelong partner?*
ALANA: *I do.*

***** RINGS PRESENTED *****

BOBBIE: *With this ring I thee wed because I love you just as you are and I look forward with great joy to spending the rest of my life with you, being with you in all that life brings. May our lives be blessed with love, laughter, and the knowing that every day in every way our lives get better and better. (Then Bobbie puts the ring on Alana's finger)*

ALANA: *With this ring I thee wed and take you as my lawfully wedded partner to have, hold, and cherish for all our days to come. I promise to do all within my power to make you happy, whole, and complete. May our lives be blessed with love, laughter, and the knowing that every day in every way our lives get better and better. (Then Alana puts the ring on Bobbie's finger)*

PREACHER: *This couple has come together in holy wedlock by pledging their love to one another by the giving and receiving of a ring, therefore, I pronounce they are joined in the name of the Father, and of the Son, and of the Holy Spirit. Then the preacher says a prayer followed by the words: "YOU MAY KISS YOUR PARTNER"*

12/31/08 Getting Married

****

The ceremony was short so immediately following the ceremony we headed to Frankfort. Our first stop was the Kentucky Retirement Systems Office to have Alana added to my health insurance. I signed the visitor's roster then we took a seat in the empty waiting area to be called back to speak with a Retirement Consultant. Before long a young girl came out, picked up the roster, looked directly at Alana and said, "Mr. Thompson," please come with me.

Alana and I just looked at one another and smiled as we followed her back to her small office. She sat behind her desk, again looked directly at Alana and said, "Well, Mr. Thompson, how can I help you?"

I spoke up, "We've just gotten married so we need to change to a family plan insurance policy."

"I see," the young girl said as she continued looking toward Alana, "Congratulations. So you're here to add your new wife to your insurance policy."

I'm the one who spoke up again and said, "No, I'm Bobbie Thompson and I'm here to add my spouse to my insurance policy."

"Oh, I'm sorry," she said as she turned my direction with a surprised look on her face. "Whenever we add a new spouse to an existing insurance policy it's usually the husband adding the wife. So, Bobbie, you're the retiree?"

"Yes."

"Ok, then we'll need for you to complete these papers indicating your spouse's name, social security number, and birth date."

"Gladly," I smiled to myself as I filled out the papers. As I handed the completed papers back to the young lady I said, "If you think you were already confused, wait until you see the name on these papers."

She read the papers and with a puzzled look on her face looked first at Alana then at me then back at Alana then read the name aloud, "Alana Nicole Sholar." She looked back at Alana again and asked, "OK, so YOUR name is Alana Nicole Sholar?"

Alana just smiled real big and said, "That's right."

I couldn't help but laugh out loud as I said, "See, I told you it would get even more confusing."

The young lady put the papers on her desk, threw up both hands, and said, "I don't even need to know."

She completed processing the papers, told us 'Congratulations,' and showed us to the door.

Our next stop was at the Unemployment Office. We'd just gotten married, had confused the girl at the Retirement Office, and were laughing like crazy when we entered the building to get Alana signed up for unemployment. The guy there said, "Now, that's a sight we don't get to see in this office very often – happy people – folks usually come in here depressed because they've just lost their job."

Alan explained that we'd just gotten married earlier that day and the guy said, "And you didn't have anything better to do than to come here?"

We'd only been married a few hours, but I already knew our life together was going to be . . . **entertaining**.

08

LET THE HARD TIMES BEGIN

My work included scheduling sales presentations with various individuals. I would usually make the presentations where I called my 'office of choice' – Panera Bread in Regency Center in Lexington.

During a presentation one morning I saw the back of a tall man as he walked past me. I thought, *"That sure looks like Tom Welch,"* a man I'd been secretary to some 15 or so years ago in the Kentucky Department of Education. I said to my customer, "Do you mind if I excuse myself for a moment. I think I see someone I know."

He said it would be fine, so I walked up behind the tall man and tapped him on his shoulder as I said, "Excuse me sir, but are you Mr. Welch."

He said, "Yes, I . . ." then began turning in my direction. Recognition quickly set in when he saw me and he was as surprised to see me as I was him. "Bobbie, Bobbie," he said with much excitement, then looked at me hard as he continued with, "where is the rest of you? You've lost so much weight."

We chatted briefly but he was on his way out, and I was in the middle of a presentation, so we made arrangements to meet at the same place in a few days.

My HUSBAND Looks Better in Lingerie Than I Do ... DAMN IT

I was so excited about the idea of getting to 'catch up' on the happenings of the past 15 years and couldn't wait to get to tell Tom everything. The day finally arrived for us to meet and we had the best time traveling down memory lane together. Then, Tom said, "It's perfect that we've ran into one another and you have some time on your hands, because I'm in need of an assistant to do my occasional travel reimbursement forms. Are you interested in helping me out?" I loved the idea of becoming Mr. Welch's secretary again and jumped at the opportunity.

****

Alan and I continued our 'positive thinking' practices of reading self-help books and watching movies on the subject. In February 2009 we learned about a meeting to discuss the possibility of Rev. Soni Cantrell coming to Lexington to start a 'Science of Mind' church. I knew nothing about Science of Mind except that I'd heard they followed the concept that 'we are spiritual beings having a physical experience.' Alana and I attended the meeting. The name AHAVA was chosen for our new church – AHAVA is a Hebrew word meaning 'love.' The motto for AHAVA is, "Where Love is Always the Answer." The first service of AHAVA was held in June 2009. Alana and I both became charter members of AHAVA, and I became the SEVA (sacred service or volunteer) coordinator.

I fell in love with AHAVA our very first service when Rev. Soni opened the service by saying, "We're an open and affirming community. We're here to give you food for thought, not to tell you what to think."

When we attended AHAVA Alana went presented in fem. She was so pleased that 'SHE' could go to church as her true-self, and not only feel 'accepted,' but welcomed and loved.

One Sunday after service I needed to stop at the Kroger store on the way home. There is a Kroger Super Center (where they sell everything from food to furniture) near the church. When I pulled into the parking lot I asked Alana, "So, are you going in with me?"

"I don't know," she said and I could sense she was very hesitant about getting out of the car. "Except for going to the support group meeting and attending AHAVA, I've gone out dressed in fem in public only a time or two – and I've never gone to a place like the Kroger store."

"Oh, come on," I said, "there's no time like the present to do something new."

She took a deep breath, opened her car door, and stepped out.

I stepped out of my side of the car and walked in Alana's direction. When I walk with Alan it's common for us to hold hands. When Alana and I go to AHAVA it's common for us to hold hands because everyone there is aware we are married. However, other than that day we went to the restaurant after the jewelry party, I've never really been in public with Alana in full fem presentation.

As we walked toward the store, out of instinct, I reached out to take Alana's hand, but quickly pulled back. I felt uncomfortable walking hand-in-hand in public with Alana. I felt like it would draw more attention to 'us,' and more particularly, 'her' if folks saw two women walking in public hand-in-hand – and I know 'attention' is something Alana would rather avoid.

Also, when I'm in public with 'Alan' it's easy to say, 'Honey' when I want his attention. But just like I'd felt uncomfortable holding Alana's hand because she was presenting in fem, I was also uncomfortable saying 'Honey' to get 'her' attention. I quickly had to adjust to calling her by name, saying Alana to get her attention, in order for *ME* to feel comfortable.

As someone who is shy will sometimes do, Alana held her head down as we walked into the store. It was as if she didn't look up and see people, then maybe they wouldn't see her either. I kept whispering to her, "Hold your head up." After a bit she realized no one was really paying that much attention to her anyway, so she began holding her head up and acting less 'self-conscious.' She soon became comfortable walking around looking at things just for the fun of it. Within minutes she transformed her stance from one of trying to hide herself, to strutting her stuff comfortably as a 'beautiful woman,' walking through the store with her head held high. I deliberately delayed picking up the items I'd come after just so we could spend a little time 'window shopping' to give Alana more time to have the experience of being in public, in the Kroger store, in broad daylight, in fem.

When we got back into the car Alana said, "Thanks baby for making me go in with you. I've never gone into a store dressed before. I did it. I feel good."

I smiled and said, "I knew you could do it."

****

In September 2009 Alan's dad was killed in an auto accident. His focus for the remainder of 2009 was on being with his mom – helping her find a place to live – and getting her moved and settled into her new apartment. Before we knew it, it was already 2010.

A couple months into 2010, once things had settled down a bit Alan began writing. When I asked him what he was doing he said, "I've had so many people tell me I should write a book about my life. About all the wrecks I've had that should have killed me but didn't. About training to become a jockey in my late teens and my terrible accident on the track. About my years of playing in the band, getting hooked on drugs, drinking and having a sex addiction. But I've never been able to write my 'whole' story because of keeping Alana a secret. Now that I've come out, I think I'm ready to write my story."

"That's cool," I said, "Can't wait to read it."

Alan wrote the story of his childhood on the farm with his brothers as they were growing up and he'd laugh as he'd share a memory triggered by his writing. He even wrote about his brother, Ricky, taking a picture of him when he was only 8-years old dressed in his mother's clothes and how he'd felt when that happened. He got the picture from his mother so I could see what he'd been talking about. He'd smile when he told me about his experiences training to be a jockey and believing his childhood dream of riding thoroughbreds on the track was coming true.

After several months of writing he began sharing about that point in his life where the battle to hide Alana had become so fierce. He was writing about his sexual confusion – about being ashamed to admit he might be gay – about not understanding what was going on with him but knowing he couldn't tell anyone – about having to be a 'man' for his wife who knew nothing of 'Alana's' existence – about the life-threatening health problems caused by keeping his true-self hidden yet being afraid to admit even to his doctor how he felt inside – about making the decision to either die or admit how he felt – about the fear he faced by coming out to his wife and family – about being diagnosed with HIV within a couple months of coming out.

I began seeing a change in Alan. All he wanted to do was sleep all the time. He'd lost his energy, his charisma, and something I never would have dreamed he'd ever lose – he lost his sex drive. We'd gone from acting like teenagers every night to rarely ever touching one another. If we had sex once a month we were doing good. He just moped around the house acting, as my mom used to say, "Like dead lice wouldn't fall off him."

I had only seen and been aware of an outgoing, charismatic, funny, energetic, wonderful person. I couldn't understand how all of a sudden Alan wanted to do nothing more than lay on the couch. It became rare for him to go anywhere with me, not even to go get the groceries. Sometimes, on those rare days that we called 'good,' he'd attempt to go out with me, but often such attempts would only result in a panic attack and we'd have to go back home. How could this person possibly be the same aggressive man who I had known for so long.

"Writing my book has taken me back. It's as if I'm back there again – in hiding – afraid someone will find out. This was my life in the past. This IS how I lived much of my life. Depressed. Fearful. Hiding myself from the world. But I thought that was all behind me. Writing my memories has brought all those old feelings back. It's as if I'm right back there again, having those same experiences, those same doubts, those same feelings of worthlessness all over again."

Writing the memoir literally knocked him off his feet. I recognized the depression from my experiences with Little Redneck, and it scared me. Alan spent a lot of time napping on the couch and wouldn't talk to me very much. Often when he did it would usually just be in response to a question I'd ask – and no matter what question I asked his answer was usually, 'it doesn't matter' or 'I don't care' so I soon came to the conclusion there was no purpose for me asking questions if I wasn't going to get an answer anyway. With Little Redneck I'd made myself sick trying to 'lift him out of the pits of darkness.' I wanted so badly to be able to 'fix it' for Alan too, but my lesson with Little Redneck had taught me the 'fixing' wasn't up to me. Alan could only be 'fixed' by taking the steps to do so himself. But Little Redneck had chosen suicide over taking steps to get better.

Those times when Alan was sulky and quiet I'd ask, "Are you mad at me for some reason?"

"No," he'd answer, usually rather sharply without offering any explanation for his behavior.

"Well, if you're telling me the truth and your behavior is the result of being depressed, there's nothing *'I'* can do to bring you out of your depression. And, if you really are angry with me, I've given you the chance to discuss it but you've chosen not to, so that's out of my hands as well. I'm here if you need me, but I can't do it for you." Then I'd just walk away to do whatever it was that needed my attention and allow him to 'be' whatever it was he needed to be. So many times I'd think of John Lennon's song, *"Let It Be,"* yet, it wasn't an easy thing to do.

Occasionally Alan would have a good day and we'd talk. Often he'd say to me, "I don't know what happens. I'll be feeling just fine then all of a sudden I can feel myself going down. It's like all of a sudden I don't have the energy to put one foot in front of the other."

All I could do was let him know I was there when he was ready to talk. It wasn't easy for me to simply 'let go and let God' take care of the situation, but I knew that was the choice I had to make. I felt thankful to Little Redneck for giving me the life lessons I needed to be able to handle this experience with Alan.

Dealing with Alan's depression was difficult. I hated seeing him the way he was, yet, at the same time, felt I had no support with anything going on in our lives – I lacked a 'husband,' a 'partner,' a 'spouse' – someone to share life with – someone to stand 'with' me – someone for 'me' to lean on. It didn't matter to me how Alan/Alana chose to present – in masculine or feminine – but it did matter to me that he/she wasn't even there due to the depression.

Right in the middle of all this, in mid-July 2010, my mom was put into the hospital. She'd been in poor health for years and I had the feeling she would never return home from this particular hospital visit. I was correct. On July 31st she passed away. I know Alan tried his best to 'be there for me' during all this, but, at times, I felt like he was leaning on me more than I was able to lean on him for support . . . and I hated being in that position. Alan was down most of the time due to depression . . . and I felt like my world was caving in on me.

Alan continued writing and experiencing deep depression with fewer and fewer good days. I edited as he wrote and put his memories in chronological order, but we had a couple events in the Fall of 2010 that absolutely required our attention. In September Alan's son got married, then in October my daughter got married.

Finally, Alan said, "I think my book is finished. I don't want to write any more." A few weeks later, after no longer being faced with the task of writing and re-living the past, he began feeling somewhat better and we decided to try another venture out of the house. I had an appointment with Mr. Welch at Panera Bread and Alan decided to go with me. When we arrived we saw that Mr. Welch had brought a friend, Jeff, along with him who was visiting from Michigan. We made our introductions, Alana being introduced as Alana as we always do when meeting new people. As is his normal practice when I meet with Mr. Welch at Panera Bread, he handed me his Panera Bread gift card and said, "Here, get whatever you want."

I asked Alana what she wanted and as I walked off to get our coffees I heard her say, "Well, Tom, I've finally finished writing my book."

When I got back from ordering our coffees Alana said, "Honey, Jeff here is just getting started in the publishing business. He's interested in taking a look at my book."

"Cool," I said as I placed Alana's cup on the table. "Well, Jeff, I'm not sure if Alana told you, but we're the type of people who believe God sends you what you need when you need it? I guess it was just meant for Alana to feel like coming out today – the very day that Tom decides to bring you along for our brief visit."

Jeff smiled as he said, "We think along the same lines then."

My HUSBAND Looks Better in Lingerie Than I Do ... DAMN IT

By the time we'd parted company with Tom and Jeff that morning we were excited about the possibility of getting Alana's book published. Alana had finished writing and we had been presented with our first step toward making it actually become a book – this time it was easy for me to recognize my 'God provided stepping stone,' or what some people call just a 'coincidence' that we had been brought together. Alana was happy, I was happy, and it looked like this just might be the ticket to helping Alana escape the grips of depression.

In early 2011 we had a conference call with Jeff after he'd had the opportunity to read Alana's manuscript. He shared some 'food for thought' with us regarding the book and we agreed that although the book contains valuable information, it just wasn't quite where it needed to be to properly convey Alana's message, which would require re-writes.

Alana went to rewriting, and I went back to editing. Before long the depression was even worse than it had been before. In our next session with Marcie she recommended Alana also start seeing a psychiatrist. At the very first visit with the psychiatrist Alana was diagnosed with severe depression and social anxiety and put on medication.

Around June 2011, I got a phone call from my sister Mitzi. As a real estate title abstractor, she owns her own company. She said, "Bobbie, a company from California contacted me about gathering some real estate data from the local courthouse, but my workload is heavy so I'm too busy. I told them you might be interested and would give them a call if you are. Here's the guy's name and phone number."

I thanked her for the lead and immediately made the call. By the time the conversation ended, I'd negotiated a 1099 Contract Labor position with the company. I was excited to have something to give my attention to other than watching Alan go through depression as we worked on re-writing his book.

Because it is a contract labor position, I have the freedom to set my own hours of work and what days I choose to work. Most days I'd get up and spend a couple hours in the morning doing things like taking some time for meditation then checking my emails and Facebook before heading out to work. On those days I do work I'd spend maybe four or five hours away from the house. When I'd leave the house in the morning Alan would be on his second or third cup of coffee trying to 'bring himself to life.' When I'd return home from work I'd usually find him napping on the couch. There was evidence that he had actually done something during the day – like washing the dishes and making the bed – but, more often than not, all I SAW was him in a depressed mode and just sitting or lying on the couch – without me – without his arms around me – holding me – sharing with me – loving me like he had when he first moved in.

Often times I'd be reminded of movies I'd watched that had scenes from inside a mental institution. Just like those people depicted as 'crazies' in the movies, I'd see Alan staring off into space with a blank look on his face and knew he wasn't 'here' with me but off in some imagined world someplace where I didn't exist. His mouth would be moving as if carrying on a conversation with someone, only that conversation was in his head. Occasionally his words would become audible and I'd say, "What did you say?" and often times I'd have to ask again, "Honey, did you say something," before I could get his attention. Most times he'd jump as if I had just woke him from a deep sleep, then I'd ask again, "Did you say something?"

Once I'd been able to gain his attention, he'd 'come back into this moment' to answer my question by saying, "No, I didn't say anything." So my next question would be, "What were you thinking about." Usually he'd just shake his head and answer, "nothing," yet within minutes he'd be sitting there staring off into space, once again engrossed in his own private world leaving me behind, carrying on conversations and having thoughts I was never privy to.

I felt so alone, and the most frustrating thing was knowing there wasn't a damned thing I could do about it. I felt as if I were carrying everything on my shoulders. I felt like I was trying to have a relationship, to live a life, with someone who only sporadically participated in that life. Our life had turned into something that didn't even resemble those wonderful days of us never being able to get enough of one another, those days of talking incessantly, those days of sharing life together. Alan was depressed, and I was sad. How I longed to have the person back that I had known for so many years and married. The person who has an outgoing charismatic personality – a sexual energy I can't resist – who is fun – dependable – supportive. I could care less whether the person was a male or a female – I just longed to have the person back.

By the end of 2011 we had finished the final manuscript for Alana's book and submitted it to Jeff. After a couple months, and a few more edits, Jeff sent me the 'printer's proof' of *"Hung in the Middle: A Journey of Gender Discovery"* (ironically the acronym for 'Hung in the Middle' turns out to be 'HIM,' a fact that never dawned on us prior to publication.) I'd typed every word in that book. I knew every memory Alana had shared. I'd lived a good many of the experiences shared in that book. However, I had never read the book from cover to cover until I received the printer's proof. It amazed me. I couldn't believe the emotion I felt reading Alana's story. There would be times that I'd laugh out loud. There would be times when tears ran down my face. I'd known Alan/Alana for nearly 30 years, but I never 'put it all together' until I read the book. I was so very proud of Alana for sharing herself with the world.

The proof was okayed, the website with Alana's "Interview with the Author," video was launched (www.hunginthemiddle.com), and the book was released in May 2012.

09

OH, THERE YOU ARE

Of course, with the release of *"Hung in the Middle: A Journey of Gender Discovery"* we wanted to make the world aware of the book's existence so I began researching marketing and promotional possibilities. I quickly realized it takes money, lots and lots of money, for marketing and promotion – and since I provided the only household income, money for marketing was something we don't have. I also learned that one way to promote a new book is by the author participating in book signing events. Because of experiencing deep depression and being diagnosed with social anxiety, we wondered if Alana would be able to face such events.

Alan walked out of a session with his psychiatrist and handed me a prescription as he said, "This is a prescription for a performance enhancement drug." I smiled broadly as I took the sheet of paper and he smiled and continued by saying, "Not THAT kind of performance enhancement. It's something to help me deal with the social anxiety at book signings." Even though it wasn't the type of 'performance enhancement' I had initially hoped, I still smiled because I understood discussing book signings with the psychiatrist as a step toward helping with the depression problem.

I continued seeking affordable ways for us to get the word out about the book when a friend of ours, Jean Marie, said to me, "You should check out the transgender conferences."

My immediate response was, "Transgender CONFERENCES? They have CONFERENCES for this stuff."

"Sure," she said, "They have them practically year round at various locations across the United States. I think there's one in Chicago soon. Google it, I'm sure you'll find what you need."

I went to Google and learned about the Chicago 'Be-All.' I saw there was an author by the name of Renee James who would be launching her new book, *"Coming Out Can Be Murder,"* at the 2012 Be-All. I thought, *"I must be on the right track if another author is launching their book at this conference."* I sent an inquiry from the 'contact' page on the Be-All website and it was Renee James herself who responded to my inquiry. Ms. James shared that it was too late for us to get involved with the Be-All Conference (which was held during the last few days in May), but, she suggested I check into the Southern Comfort Conference scheduled for September.

When I got Renee's response I said to Alana, "Honey, do you know anything about an event called Southern Comfort Conference? It's been suggested that we attend that if possible as a way of promoting *"Hung in the Middle."*

Her eyes lit up as if she were a child and I had just said, "Santa Claus is coming today to see only you," and she said, "Sure I know about Southern Comfort Conference. I'd love to attend Southern Comfort – I've dreamed of going to Southern Comfort."

"You've never said anything to me about it. Actually, I didn't even know there were such things as transgender conferences until Jean Marie mentioned it."

"I've never said anything because I never thought it would ever be something you'd want to go to."

"Well, if we can come up with the funds, I think there might be a chance we can go this year to promote your book." That same 'kid expecting a special visit all her own from Santa Claus' look came across her face again, and I swear I saw her jump up and down a couple times as she clapped her hands and giggled gleefully – I might have just been imagining the jumping and hand clapping, but she was happy.

I was so impressed that Renee James had not only replied to my inquiry about Be-All, but had also made a recommendation on how to proceed in my search for places to promote "HIM," and decided to visit her website (www.reneejamesauthor.com) to learn about her book. I ordered the book from her website and Renee even signed it for me. I LOVED IT. The main character, Bobbi, (a name I'm quite fond of), is a transgender woman who is somewhat confused as to what best 'fits' her situation – bi-sexual, gay, or trans – and eventually discovers that 'woman' is the best fit. At the same time, Bobbi is involved in a mystery regarding the death of her friend.

As I read about Bobbi's feelings and lack of clarity as to her 'best fit' it was as if things Alana had shared with me about her search of gender discovery were being confirmed because someone else was having the same experiences. And, just like when I read the printer's proof for *"Hung in the Middle,"* as I read *"Coming Out..."* there were times when I laughed out loud, and times when a tear would slide down my cheek. One big difference, however, was how literally 'pissed off' I felt because of the way the transwomen in *"Coming Out . . ."* were treated.

We decided to have Alana's first book signing at the 5th Annual Lexington Kentucky Pride Festival on June 30, 2012. We purchased a white canopy and had the words "Hung in the Middle" printed around each of the four sides. Alana was dressed en-fem, popped a performance enhancement pill a time or two through the day, and talked with people all day long – including Lexington's Mayor, Jim Gray, an openly gay man. We even had a few folks come to us and say, "What is 'Hung in the Middle' – is this porn?" We laughed and said, "Well, there are some sexual situations included in the book, but it's a memoir." It felt good seeing the spirit coming back to Alana as that wonderful charismatic, outgoing, jovial personality of hers shined and drew people near. "Oh, there you are," I thought as I watched her from a distance.

Alana had wonderful family support at her first book signing with her mom, sister, and nephew coming out to join us. My friend, Vallarie, even came out and spent some time with us. At one point I looked up and my son and his girlfriend were walking toward our canopy – at a GLBT event – the area's LARGEST GLBT event – Pride Fest. Having the support of Alana's family is wonderful, but seeing my son come out in support of Alana said so much to me about his acceptance – a far cry from his initial unfounded fears.

The first book signing had been in a location where Alana felt comfortable coming dressed en-fem – among the GLBT population – at a GLBT event. However, the next book signing was scheduled to be held at a local bookstore. It was obvious that Alana was facing some fears when it came to the prospect of attending her next book signing.

In anticipation of the event she said to me, "Honey, I know I've got these little pills to help me through these book signings and I think I did just fine at the Pride Festival, however, you know I haven't been in the general public dressed en-fem but once or twice in my life. I hope I can do this."

"Honey, you can do anything you put your mind to. All you have to do is want to do it. You're written the book that tells the world who you are. All you're doing now is letting folks see who you are. And, isn't that something you've wanted all your life? Haven't you always wanted folks to 'see' Alana? So see a woman?"

The day arrived for the event and Alana got all dressed up. We got to the parking lot of the book store and I parked the car. Alana reached into her purse and pulled her bottle of little pills out and put a couple in her hands. "Didn't you take a couple of those already?"

"I did," she said, "But I think I'm going to need a couple more."

She popped the pills into her mouth, took a drink of her Coke, and quickly blew out a breath as she reached for her car door. "It's now or never," she said as she opened the door and got out of the car.

When we entered the store, we learned that particular day was a day when patrons could 'exchange' their old books for credit to buy new books. The place was packed – the aisles were crowded with people. I walked up to the counter and told the clerk we were there for the book signing and she immediately got the store manager for us. The store manager was very kind and set up our table for the signing near the entrance to the store.

Although the store was packed with people, very few even so much as looked our direction. Everyone was so involved with exchanging their books and browsing for new ones that hardly anyone approached our table to ask about Alana's book – a few did, but it was very few. I noticed the occasional 'stolen glance' in our direction, but no one said anything derogatory to us.

Alana's mom had come to the book signing with us to once again show her support. We hadn't been there long when friends began showing up who had been unable to come, or maybe even uncomfortable with coming, to the book signing at the Pride Fest. The big surprise that day was when my sister, Mitzi, showed up, and she had both her daughters with her.

Although Alana had initially shown hesitation about presenting en-fem in a public place that had nothing to do with the GLBT community, once she was surrounded by so many friends and loved ones, I could tell she was comfortable with her surroundings and enjoying talking about her book.

Later after the book signing I asked Mitzi, "Well, how did you feel seeing 'Alana' for the first time."

She said, "I wondered about how I might feel when I was on my way to the store. You talked about how freaked out you were when you all went to the Mall that day, so I wondered if I'd be freaked out too. But I wasn't. It was just Alan . . . the same person I've always known."

"Humph," I thought, *"I wonder now why I was so freaked out that day."* Then it dawned on me, *"I was freaked out because when I saw Alana for the first time, Alan had never mentioned Alana existed. Mitzi, on the*

other hand, had been prepared to see Alana. I never had the opportunity to prepare."

****

Part of our marketing endeavors included social media. Alana set up a fan page on Facebook so I decided to set up my own Facebook and Twitter pages. I set them up as "Alana's Spouse" to be able to tie in my connection with Alana and her book. I started receiving Facebook friend requests from everywhere and 95% or more of the requests are from trans-persons. *"Where have all these people been hiding,"* I thought. I had no idea the transgender population even existed, yet I accumulated a few hundred friends in no time.

I came across some statistics that said '1 out of every 100' people living in the United States fits under the 'transgender' umbrella. I thought, *"1 out of 100, that's only 1% and 1% of anything isn't very much."* Then I looked up the population for the United States. I found information on a census that said there were 315-MILLION people in the USA in mid-2011. I did the calculations and found that would mean there are over 3Million transgender persons here in the USA – and many of my Facebook friend requests have come from other countries, so if there could be 3Million trans-persons in the USA, then God only knows how many there are in the world. All of a sudden that 1% looked much bigger to me.

Then I thought about the number of people just here in this small town of Versailles, Kentucky. We have a population of around 8,000 people. *"Crap,"* I thought, *"if 1 out of every 100 people living here were trans, we'd have 80 transgender people here – that's a pretty big number for such a small town."* I do know there are other trans-persons here in Versailles because I've met a few since getting with Alana. But I had no idea there were any transgender persons in Versailles because they lived their lives 'in secret' like Alana had done for so many years.

Then I started to break it down even further by wondering how many students attend Woodford County Schools – so I went back to Google to see if I could find that information. I couldn't find the number enrolled in Woodford County Schools totally, but I did find the enrollment for the high school, which was 1,230 students – and given these statistics, that could mean 12 students are walking the halls of Woodford County High School who could be having the same fearful experiences as Alan was having when he walked those same halls. And those statistics were for the "trans" (or just the "T" part) of the GLBT population. Knowing this made my heart ache.

When I got around to starting my Twitter account I thought it would be 'cute' to post the question, "Is it just me or is there anyone else out there who married a man who turned out to be a woman?" One of the names Twitter suggested I follow was Buck Angel (www.buckangel.com). I thought, *"that name sounds familiar,"* so I Googled the name. Once I saw his picture and read a little about him, I remembered watching an interview with Buck about starting his own adult film company because 'main stream' companies thought the world wasn't ready for a man without his junk, – apparently the main stream companies were wrong. I believe there is a healthy place for adult films (in the lives of ADULTS) and admired Buck for refusing to take 'no' for an answer, so I started following him on Twitter. To my surprise, within minutes he followed me back. I told him about Alana's book and he said he would read it.

Occasionally he'd read about a particular experience Alana had shared and then send me a message regarding his thoughts on that experience. First, I couldn't believe that Buck Angel, with his extremely busy schedule, was taking time to read Alana's book, but to take time to share his comments with me, WOW, that simply blew me away. I had been impressed with Buck Angel when I saw the interview, now, for the second time I was impressed with Buck Angel.

We were saving our pennies as fast and furiously as we could as the deadline for registering to attend the Southern Comfort Conference approached much too quickly. Fortunately we were successful in coming up with the funds, and I took care of our conference registration and lodging reservations. Not much after getting everything taken care of I got a message from Buck that said, "Hey, I just found out I'll be attending the Southern Comfort Conference." Now it was my turn to act like a kid who had just been told Santa Claus was on his way to visit because I knew this could be my chance to finally meet Buck Angel.

Since we would be selling *"Hung in the Middle"* at Southern Comfort Conference, I asked Buck if I could say something like, "Buck likes the book," in our promotional material. I was once again impressed with his kindness when his reply read, "You can say I loved the book and think it will help so many people struggling to become themselves. Thanks to Alana's bravery." I just keep on being impressed by this person.

10

A GG AT SCC

September 2012 finally arrived and we headed to Atlanta, Georgia for the Southern Comfort Conference. I was excited yet a bit apprehensive because I knew I was stepping into a brand new world for me that I knew very little about – except for what I'd experienced with Alana. Much of what I did know I'd learned from our long talks while lying on the couch when we first got together and from helping with her book.

I did what I usually do, which is jump in with both feet, so we signed up to participate in the 'stuffing party' which is where volunteers arrive early to put together the conference attendee packets. Alana and I arrived in the room where the 'party' was taking place and the room was already full of people. As I first glanced around the room, I didn't see any other genetic women there. Because *"I"* was the one who was different I felt a bit out of place. I immediately had the thought, *"this must be how a transperson feels when they step into a room full of genetic-persons."* Then I thought, *"How bizarre. If someone were looking through the window into this room they might think I'm the only 'normal' person in the room, rather than the 'oddball' – how wrong they would be – what an oddball I am at this moment."*

In this room full of trans-persons, some male-to-female and some female-to male, I began feeling a little uncomfortable again because in my vocabulary I still have no word to express the mixing of two genders, like the cocoon stage of the butterfly. But I wasn't uncomfortable for very long. From what little time I'd spent with other transgender persons by attending the support group meetings with Alana, I'd learned to identify the gender of a person based on the method of their dress. I'd learned, if the person is dressed as or is presenting as a male, then it is proper for me to identify, or recognize, or address that person as male and use the pronouns he or him. Likewise, if the person is dressed as or presenting as a female, then it is proper for me to identify, or recognize, or address that person as female and use the pronouns she or her. Having this knowledge through being educated by attending the support group meetings with Alana made it easier for me to properly identify and know how to address each person in the room. Identifying the gender being presented by each person allowed me to see that person as that gender. I likened what I was experiencing in that room at that moment to attending a drag show and recognizing the person on stage as a woman ... I saw, or identified, or recognized each person in the room as the gender they presented. I saw the women as women and the men as men.

The experience reminded me of those pictures that were popular back in the day where when you first look at the picture you have no idea what you're looking at, but, as you change your focus, your perspective and look deeper into the picture, then the 'hidden' picture comes out. Once you've found the perspective that shows you what's behind the initial confusion or chaos and you see the 'real' picture, then it's difficult to go back to seeing the confusion. What's inside is easily identified each time you look at the picture from then on just like once I perceived the persons presenting as male to be male, and the females as females, that was all I could see.

In a matter of minutes I was comfortable and smiled, saying 'hello' to people as they'd look my direction. Some said 'hello' back to me, some nodded a hello, some smiled, and some quickly looked away. I wasn't sure if they didn't want me looking at them, or if they didn't want to look at me. I quickly found a person in charge, introduced myself and Alana, and said, "We're here to help. What do you want us to do."

She pointed to a table in the room with materials laid out in a certain order and a parade of people walking around it picking up one of each of the items and placing it in a large envelope. Then she said, "Well, I think we can use one more person here," as she led me to the table and made a place for me among the walkers. Alana had already began a conversation with someone as soon as we walked into the room, so, since there was no room at the table for her anyway, she took a seat across the room chatting with the person she had just met.

"I'm very familiar with this type of work," I thought as I remembered collating and stuffing packets for various conferences back in the day when I worked for Kentucky Department of Education. I paid attention to what I was doing and didn't look up very often because I didn't want anyone to think I was staring at them. Try-

ing to make eye contact only to be avoided made me feel uncomfortable. In trying to be open to the people in the room, I felt like I was making them uncomfortable rather than achieving my intent, which was to make them more comfortable. Before long one of the table walkers spoke up, "I think you're one of my Facebook friends. Aren't you, Alana's Spouse?"

"Yes, I am," I said looking up as I continued to pick up the items from the table and stuff them into an envelope. "My name is Bobbie."

"I thought that was you," she said. "I'm Trudy."

I had enjoyed a chat with Trudy just a few nights before via Facebook and was relieved she had spoken up. "Oh, we chatted a few nights ago, didn't we?" I asked as we all continued to walk the circle around the table.

"Yes we did. Is this your first trans conference?"

"Yes it is. Actually, up until a couple months ago I didn't even know there was any such thing as a transgender conference – and not until 2006 did I know there was any such thing as being transgender."

A smile crossed her face as she said, "Be prepared, you're in for a total mind fuck."

A few of the other girls laughed slightly then someone else spoke up and said, "Hi Bobbie. We're Facebook friends too. I'm Stephanie."

I said hello to Stephanie, then a few more of the ladies in the room began introducing themselves to me. All my inhibitions quickly disappeared as I made a whole room full of new friends.

The next day was Princess Day. We were told that part of the reason for Princess Day is to help some of the attendees acclimate to presenting en-fem, in other words, wearing a dress, panty hoses, heels, etc., as a woman. Many attendees had never been in public dressed en-fem before. Although Alana has explained to me she considers herself 'fem' at all times because she is always who she is and always wears ladies underwear, ladies jeans, and the same t-shirts I wear, I was aware of Alana's limited experiences of being in public wearing a dress, pantyhose, heels, etc., and knew how fearful she had been on a few occasions when she had done so. My heart went out to these ladies knowing that many of them were most likely experiencing the same fear and anxiety Alana had experienced on such occasions.

I decided I wanted to personally do something to make each person I met feel more at ease, more comfortable. So, instead of walking with my head down in order to not make eye contact with anyone, I began looking directly at as many people as I could when we'd pass. Often they would look straight ahead as if they didn't want to make eye contact with me, but, for those who would look my direction, I'd smile and say, "Hi Hun."

Occasionally they'd smile back at me, and say, "Hi." I could feel a change in the energy around us as if we both somehow became more relaxed. That was often the only contact I might have with that person the entire time I'd be at the conference, but, I felt as if I had played some part, even if it were ever so slight, in making their experience of presenting en-fem in public a bit more enjoyable, whether that was their first time to do so, or if they had done so thousands of times.

Princess Day was a wonderful experience. We started out with a manicure and pedicure for Alana. It didn't dawn on me that I could have one too so I spent my time taking pictures of Alana as she was having the time of her life being a girl – and I got great pleasure seeing the smiles of happiness on her face. The next item on the day's agenda was a make-over at Sephora Cosmetics followed by all the Princesses getting together for lunch. I looked around the restaurant at all the smiling faces; all the ladies chatting up a storm, enjoying one another's company – just like any other luncheon I'd ever attended that involved a multitude of ladies.

The next day we took our books down to the SCC marketplace to set up our vendor's table. Everyone was busy getting their displays all set up. Several of the ladies we'd met the previous day stopped by to be one of the first to purchase a book and get Alana's autograph. We'd chat with each one getting to know them a little better and making new friends. Several allowed us to take their picture with Alana and gave us permission to include them on the www.hunginthemiddle.com website.

As the day went on more and more people began arriving for the conference and would stroll through the marketplace to check things out. At one point a very attractive man was strolling through and caught my eye. He caught me looking at him, so I nodded and he nodded back. I stood to shake hands with him and said, "Hi, I'm Bobbie, but most folks know me as Alana's Spouse," as I pointed toward Alana's direction.

"Nice to meet you Bobbie," he said, "My name is Tyson."

We chatted for quite some time and for some reason I felt drawn to him – such a pleasant person – so very attractive – and somehow our conversation included briefly talking about our common beliefs in positive thinking and the concept that 'we are one.' After a bit we said our good-byes and he walked away. I walked back to Alana and said, "Honey, did you see that man I was just talking to?"

"No, I'm sorry, I was busy chatting over here with a couple customers."

"You'd like him. Very handsome, and very much a positive thinker. I'm glad he strolled into this room to look around. I guess other hotel guests can come into the marketplace and look around to see all the things for sale even if they're not here for the conference."

Another customer came up and got Alana's attention so I picked up the conference's program guide to try to map out the sessions of interest to me. As I was flipping through the guide I saw Tyson's picture ... he was a conference presenter, and I hadn't even realized he was a transman.

As soon as Alana's customer walked away I very excitedly showed her Tyson's picture and said, "Honey, look, this is the person I was talking to. He's a transman and I didn't even know it. I thought I was just talking to a man."

"You were," Alana said, "You were excited about talking with him and even found him attractive. But now that you realize you can put 'trans' in front of 'man' does that make your conversation with him any less enjoyable, what he had to say any less valid, or make him any less attractive?"

"No, of course not," I responded sharply because her question almost pissed me off.

"Then why are you so excited about pointing out to me that he was trans?"

"I don't know. It just surprised me I guess. I couldn't tell the difference. I thought I was talking to a man."

Again Alana said, "YOU WERE. You were just talking to a man. That's the point. Transmen ARE men, and transwomen ARE women. It's only because others perceive us as something other than what we are that causes the confusion and difficulties."

I finally understood the point she was trying to get across. People are what they are – the prefix of 'trans' prior to the gender is simply another label to give 'us' some degree of understanding – a way of trying to get something that is uncommon to 'us' to make sense to 'us.'

Later that evening Alana and I were once again in the marketplace where she was selling and signing books when one of our new friends, Kimmy, came to me and said, "I just saw your friend, Buck Angel, walk into the bar."

I was on my way to the bar in a flash. I saw Buck from a distance and I guess you could say I 'ran him down.' I finally got close enough to tap him on the shoulder and he turned around to face me. I held out my hand and said, "Hi Mr. Angel, I'm Bobbie, aka Alana's spouse."

He shook my hand as he said, "Yes, I recognize you. So glad to finally meet you. Is Alana with you?"

"She's at our vendor's booth in the marketplace."

"I'll be heading that way soon. I'm looking forward to meeting her. But right now I have a few people in here I need to talk with."

"No problem. I know you're busy. I'm just glad we're finally able to meet."

"Me too," he said, then we both turned and I walked back to the marketplace to Alana.

After a short period of time Buck walked into the vendors' area and made his way over to our table. He suggested we get a picture with the three of us together with him holding the book, so we did. After that picture was taken I handed the book to Alana and everyone laughed as I pushed her out of the next picture and gave BUCK ANGEL a kiss. As far as I was concerned my whole conference had just been made. I couldn't imagine anything else could possibly happen that could make it better. Buck stayed and chatted with us for a few minutes and my initial impression that he is one of the kindest sweetest people I've ever met held true.

****

I had been invited to and looked forward to getting to go to the 'Comfort Zone,' a meeting for the genetic spouses of male-to-female transgender persons. The few days I'd been at the conference I'd felt like an 'outsider looking in' and knew I'd finally be getting to spend some time with others who are like 'me' ... happy with the gender in which they were born.

There were approximately 10 women who attended the spouses meeting, which was moderated by a psychologist. I wasn't in the room for very long when I found I was still an 'outsider looking in' in this room full of spouses of transwomen. I felt as if I had absolutely nothing in common with the other spouses. Most talked about how their 'husbands' had to hide the fact they were trans – EVEN HIDING IT FROM THEIR CHILDREN – and that often the only time their spouse would get to dress was in the privacy of their own home with no one else in the world knowing the situation. Several expressed that they loved their spouses and had been together for many years (one couple had just celebrated their 40th Wedding Anniversary), therefore, they didn't want the marriage to end, and although they were doing their best to be supportive, they were within themselves having difficulty coping with the situation no matter how hard they tried. One common problem they faced was having no one else to share their experiences and concerns with except in therapy sessions.

When it came my turn to have the floor I found it difficult to speak (a rarity for me) because I didn't have the same issues. Finally, I said, "Hi, I'm Bobbie, and I'm married to Alana Nicole Sholar, who has just released her memoir entitled, *"Hung in the Middle: A Journey of Gender Discovery."* Because of Alana's book, I want to 'shout it from the rooftops' that my spouse is transgender, so, I'm not really in the same place as you ladies. The whole purpose of Alana's book is to put a spotlight on being transgender to help others who are transgender, and to teach those who are not about those who are."

I immediately felt like an oddball again. I sensed what I can only describe as a 'jealously' that I had the freedom to speak openly, not only in this room, but in public, about my transgender spouse. I began getting questions from the other wives like, "how did you feel the first time you were in public with your spouse dressed," and "did people stare at you or make nasty comments?" One question that seems to come up time and time again no matter if the people I'm around are straight, trans, or whatever, and it was asked here too, "how can you have sex with your spouse when 'he' acts so feminine?"

I answered each of their questions as best I could, but when the meeting ended I couldn't get out of that room fast enough. I was so much more comfortable being with Alana and surrounded by transpersons than I had been in a room full of GG's.

Prior to attending Saturday night's festivities, we spent the bulk of the day exchanging contact information with the many many wonderful new friends we'd made. At one time I looked up and Dr. Marci Bowers, one of the conference presenters, was entering the vendor's area. I approached her and told her she was one of Alana's favorite people and asked if she would mind taking a picture with Alana. She agreed and Alana got a chance to chat briefly with Dr. Bowers while I took the picture. Just like meeting Buck Angel had been a highlight of the conference for me (and for Alana too actually), getting to meet Dr. Bowers was one of the conference highlights for Alana.

As we got our things together on Sunday morning to leave it dawned on me that I had just spent the last five days living with a woman – with Alana. Alana and I had been together for nearly six years, and although I had begun to recognize her as a woman more and more frequently, this was really the first opportunity we'd had to be together with Alana presented fully en-fem where I totally recognized her as a woman the entire time. I had the thought, *"I've wondered if I could handle things when Alana's transition is complete and if this experience is any indication of how things will be, then I believe everything will be just fine."*

Then it dawned on me that this hadn't only been a first for us as a couple, but a first for Alana as well. There had never been a time in her life that she had gotten to live being recognized as female continuously for that length of time. Actually, there had been only a few times in her life, period, that she had presented en-fem and was seen by others as a female. Those times, of course, had been limited to the support group meetings, occasionally visiting a gay bar, going to AHAVA church, and now at the 2012 Southern Comfort Conference.

We loaded up our luggage ready to leave the hotel and when we reached the lobby it was crowded with people, mostly men, some dressed in suits, some in jeans and a t-shirt, some in slacks and a dress shirt. Most of them were also pushing carts full of luggage and checking out of the hotel. As I looked around I thought I caught a glimpse of familiarity in a face or two, but I couldn't be sure. That's when it dawned on me that of all the wonderful new friends I had made during the week, the majority of them were probably standing in front of me right now and I didn't even know who they are. I had grown to care about my new friends during what little time we'd spent together the previous few days, but suddenly realized that I didn't even know their given names. I knew the names they used during their week of presenting en-fem at the conference, but I had no idea who these people were bustling around in the lobby. I knew Alana had just had her first opportunity to be recognized as a female for a continuous period of time and, because of her book, I expected she would have more opportunities to do so. But what about the other conference attendees? How many of my new found friends had to remove their feminine persona to hide it away until the next conference or similar event gave them the opportunity to present their feminine selves once again. That thought made me sad.

As luck would have it, when Alana and I had checked out of the hotel and was standing out front waiting for our car to be brought around, Dr. Bowers was there waiting for her ride to the airport. Alana reached into her bag and pulled out one of her books and gave it to Dr. Bowers as a gift. It pleased Alana that Dr. Bowers accepted the gift and said something to the effect of 'now having reading material for her flight.'

We drove home exhausted from the events of the previous five days, but thankful for the experience. It was hard to tell which one of us had benefitted the most from the experience. I'd dare say the number is few of persons who have had the eye-opening experience of being a GG who attended a conference with their transgender spouse and had the privilege of openly sharing that experience with everyone and anyone. I thoroughly enjoyed the conference and hope there are additional such conferences in our future.

My HUSBAND Looks Better in Lingerie Than I Do ... DAMN IT

Bobbie and Alana with Buck Angel at the
2012 Southern Comfort Conference

11

SITUATIONS AND THE CIRCUMSTANCES

As more and more people become aware of Alana's memoir, she gets more and more invitations for book signings, interviews, and presentations. Of course, each invitation results in another opportunity to present enfem and be recognized as the woman she is. I've become so accustomed to **seeing** and **saying** Alana that at one point it finally dawned on me that, right before my eyes, without me even consciously recognizing the transformation, my man was becoming a woman IN MY OWN MIND.

In Alana's mind, she has been a woman her entire life – it's just that no one else was aware of that fact. To me, it's kinda like comparing it to the time when everyone thought the earth was flat. When did the earth become round? Fact is, it was always round, but it wasn't round to the people until it became round 'in their mind' – until someone else proved it to be round and their understanding or perspective changed. The earth was always what it was, but no one knew it. Everyone believed and said it was something that it was not, until they learned the truth for themselves. Kinda like I and others believed Alana was a man, until I learned the truth that she's something other than what I had always believed.

Whenever we're at home we spend much of our time wearing what we call our 'hunker down clothes,' which are our sweat pants and t-shirts. There was a time when while wearing our hunker downs, I saw a male whenever I looked at Alana, however, although I am seeing the same person, there is never a time now that I completely see a male – there is always some degree of feminine present – and, in my mind, she's taking over the masculine.

When we're in situations related to the book, which is more and more often, Alana, she, and her are the words I use when speaking about my spouse. It's getting to the point now that the only time I ever use Alan, he, or him is when we're around family or with friends who have known Alan for a lifetime and are not around Alana often enough to recognize in their mind that she is a woman. Although everyone is aware of Alana, there are a certain few who still only see Alan, and again, one can only speak from their own perspective, and one's perspective is always based on their experience – in this case, for many, seeing a male and saying Alan comes from the experience of having known Alan all their lives. When we're home alone I rarely use the name Alan ... or Alana – I say 'Sweetheart.'

Many people have asked me, "how do you do it," meaning how is it I can be married to a transgender person. But it's not whether my spouse is a man or a woman that causes the difficulties we face in our relationship – love has no gender. The things we face that puts the most strain on our relationship are dealing with Alana's depression and our financial difficulties. Although depression isn't something that most couples might have to deal with, financial difficulty is a common occurrence that causes many divorces.

Alana lost her job in 2008 when the factory where she worked closed down. Her book was released in May 2012 and we had hoped it would generate enough income to replace the income she'd lost when the factory closed. Although we're quite proud of how well her book has sold, word of mouth has been the main source of promotion thus far. It takes money that our one-income household doesn't have for marketing costs to generate the amount of sales that would give us a livable income.

When I think of my spouse, my love, Alana, I smile and am happy to have this wonderful person in my life. When I think of the issues we face caused by Alana's loss of income, overwhelming medical bills because of having been diagnosed with HIV, and the countless hours she spends lying on the couch because of depression, I confess I have had the thought, *"my life could be so much easier if I just divorce Alana."*

But, without Alana, what would life be? She brings so much love, so many experiences I otherwise could never have. So, I wipe my tears, and think about this wonderful person I share my life with, thankful she's a part of my life, and thankful for everything I've learned and the experiences I've had because of her. It's when I think of Alana, how much I love her, the wonderful experiences we've shared together that the smile comes back to my face and just like the words in Jason Mraz's song I think, "I won't give up on us." I go back to the affirmation that has helped me through so many times as I say to myself, "I have no idea how my bills will get paid this month," but I don't stop there, I continue with, "but I know they will get paid." With this knowledge the stress of debt is released and I am able to make it through another day. And somehow, the money shows up when we need it.

Because we haven't been able to afford the facial feminization surgery Alana desires she still lives life 'hung in the middle' of two genders, just like the title of her memoir indicates. However, she is always dressed en-fem because the jeans she wears are women's jeans, the t-shirts she wears are the same ones I wear, and she can sure rock a thong . . . and it totally pisses me off that my husband, ah, er, spouse looks better in lingerie than I do . . . damn it.

PART 2
LESSONS LEARNED

12

LET'S TALK ABOUT SEX, BABE

I listened to the words of desire as he spoke. I looked at his handsome face, focusing on his flawless shiny black skin. I enjoyed watching the movement of his thick lips as he pronounced each word. His African accent made the words he spoke even more exciting to me. He wasn't African-American, but African – with dark black flawless shiny skin and a heavy accent – my Literature Professor who read the poem he had assigned us to read the previous night. I had read those same words as he had instructed, but when I read them, they had only been words and held no meaning for me.

It was the way he spoke the words that caused them to come to life – words describing the beauty of the woman the poet so deeply desired. He spoke of her hair, her eyes, her mouth, her neck. That's when I noticed the snickers coming from a few of the younger students sitting in the classroom. Our Professor continued reading describing her shoulders, her arms, her breasts . . . the snickers grew louder as they became giggles. Then when he spoke the words, "give me your virginity" the low giggles became laughing out loud. It bothered me because the laughing had caused him to stop reading.

He lowered the book slowly and placed it on his desk as he looked around the room of laughing students. He said nothing for a moment, just watching as the laughing died down. The energy in the room became uncomfortable as we all sat quietly for a moment before he said in his beautiful heavy African accent, "Tell me one thing that God has given to all mankind in common. Is it skin color?" He hesitated, continuing to gaze around the room as he let his question sink in.

The class was at Kentucky State University so the skin color of the students ranged from fair-skinned blue-eyed blonds to the darkest black skinned African students and everything in between.

Without answering the first, he asked a second question, "Was it language?" Again, there was a multitude of languages presented in the room. He hesitated once again giving everyone time to take in his second question.

"How about religion? Surely religion is of extreme importance to God. Did God give all mankind one religion in common?" Again he hesitated yet never voicing the obvious answers to his questions.

"What about sex?" he asked, hesitating once more as if waiting for an answer before saying, "If sex is so important to God that He gave the gift of sex to all mankind, then I don't believe sex is something for us to laugh about, but is something to be appreciated." With that he picked the book up from the desk and finished reading the poem – and I was glad he did.

****

When someone wants to talk to me about my relationship with Alana, often times their first question is about sex. A question I was asked early in our relationship was, "Doesn't it make you feel funny when you have sex with Alana dressed like a woman?" I couldn't help but giggle a bit as I replied, "Honey, I've got news for you, when we have sex, we're both naked."

But, things have changed over time. Initially when Alan and I got together years ago I saw him as a masculine aggressive male and our sex life was very satisfying. And, it is true that when we have sex we are both naked, however, as time passes, I'm seeing my very masculine aggressive male more and more as a female. It's true that, as her book's title indicates, Alana is 'hung in the middle' of two genders – no longer a male, but not yet totally female either.

I'm very much aware my spouse is no longer the masculine aggressive male sex partner I once had. The first several times I recognized the feminine energy coming from Alana during times of intimacy I couldn't handle it. I'm aware that in my mind, I'm recognizing Alana as the woman she is, however, I don't identify as lesbian. My perspective of the person has changed right along with Alana's progression through transition. I'm losing sight of the male, and more readily recognizing a female. I love the person but didn't know how to 'make love' to the person ... but very much wanted to do so. I knew my difficulty was due to the change in my perspective of the person ... from having known only 'Alan' to now being aware of 'Alana.'

During times of intimacy to get away from identifying either a 'male' or a 'female' I decided to just close my eyes and concentrate on the 'feeling,' the energy we've always shared. That way, I don't 'see' either a male or a female, but can concentrate on just being with the 'person.' I kiss those same thick lips I've always kissed. I feel those same loving arms around me. I run my hands over my lover's body, my spouse's body, and feel the sexual energy that has always been between us. I concentrate on the touch of warm skin. As I run my hands down my love's back I give attention to the dip at the waist that's followed by mounds of buttocks and long legs. I feel the hands of the person I love as they touch me ... caress me. I feel our warm bodies against one another. I feel the energy from touching the person I love and being touched by the person I love. It's easy to lose myself in that moment, in that energy, and enjoy our satisfying sex life together.

Then I remembered something Alan said to me years ago that 'a body is a body is a body.' Now, that statement holds meaning for me. Although my perspective of the person has changed, the body is simply the container that holds the spirit from which all that energy comes. The body is just the 'package' the gift comes in. It doesn't matter if I perceive the body as a male body or a female body – it's the same package – it's just the body. When we get naked together I can see physical signs that the body before me is male. Yet, I see other physical signs that the body before me is female. I simply let both of those gender labels go and love the body and enjoy the energy it emits. It IS the same person I've always enjoyed. They ARE the same lips that have always kissed me. They ARE the same arms that have always held me. It is the same person I have always had such a satisfying sexual relationship with.

I often think about how my own body is in a state of constant change, as all bodies are. My body is no longer that of a child as it once was. My body no longer carries an extra 100 pounds as it once did. Yet, although my body goes through constant change, I am still the SAME PERSON ... as is Alana.

During the experience of simply enjoying one another there have been times when we are so lost in the energy of each other it's difficult to determine which one of us has the penis and which one of us has the vagina. The feeling, the energy is so intense that knowing which one is which is of no importance – it simply doesn't matter.

Fantasies play a big part in sex, and, I guess if it can be classified as a fantasy, I fanaticize about, or concentrate on, the way it makes me feel when I get lost in the pleasure that follows after I touch or am touched by Alana. I'm very much aware that Alana fanaticizes as well, and know she envisions herself as a female in a lesbian relationship. That's just fine with me. I can be a lesbian IN HER MIND. In MY MIND I'm not having a lesbian experience, nor am I having a straight experience. I'm having a spiritual experience, a love experience, by losing myself in the energy, losing myself in the person I genuinely love and am thoroughly enjoying.

I've had people ask me, "Is your relationship a lesbian relationship or is it a straight relationship?" My answer is, "I'm just a person in love with and married to another person." But, I've found that the answer to that question has to come from the person asking the question and their answer is always based on their perspective and how they choose to view us.

For example, those who recognize Alana as a female views us as a lesbian couple. However, there are those persons who simply can't wrap their mind around a female with a penis, therefore, they allow the penis to define our relationship, and view us as a straight couple. As for us, we don't care how others choose to define our relationship. What's important to us is that we HAVE a loving relationship.

****

Lots of girls like guys... and I've learned through my gay friends, lots of guys like guys too. I've never been able to understand the gay experience because it's never been my experience. I was with a distant relative of mine who is lesbian when I made the statement, "I can't comprehend being attracted to the same gender."

She immediately said, "I know what you mean," which confused me briefly until she continued, "Except for the love my parents share, I've never been able to understand being attracted to the opposite gender. I don't know how men and women can be attracted to one another."

That was a perspective I'd never considered before and the thought that she couldn't understand something considered by so many as the 'natural' way of being initially sounded totally bazar to me. But, what she said did make sense because I know the only way we understand anything is based on our own experiences. If I, and those who identify as straight, can have no understanding of a same gender relationship, then, it makes sense to me that anyone who has only experienced an attraction to the same gender wouldn't understand opposite gender attraction. I'd just never thought of it like that before.

But, an experience I have had, and do understand, is the experience of being a woman attracted to a man. Alana is a woman. As a woman, she is attracted to men. Alan is not a gay man. Yes, there is a difference. So, if we must label and categorize to bring understanding to situations, then I guess Alana and I would both wear the 'bi-sexual' label. Alana, because she enjoys sex with both men and women; and, me, because I have sex with a person who at one point or another in our relationship, and in my mind, has been both male and female.

Alana likes to flirt. I like to flirt. One big difference is I get to flirt in person. It's not as readily accepted for Alana to flirt with men in person as it is for me to do so – unless we happen to be at a gay bar. On those occasions, Alana gets to do a lot of flirting, and it is fun to watch her being such a girly girl (she's so much more girly than I have ever been or could ever be).

But, we rarely go out any more these days to either gay bars or straight bars, so neither one of us gets to do much flirting. However, technology has brought flirting into the home through various online dating sites. Alana said she would like to set up a profile with a couple dating sites to do some flirting, and, because I know she likes the attention – and what woman doesn't – I had no problem with it. She wound up setting up a profile at two different sites ... one site geared toward the general public, and the other geared toward the transgender population. She dressed in several of her sexy outfits and lingerie and we took a few pictures and added them to both sites. Then we decided to make some very provocative 'mini-movies' (starring Alana only) and added them to both sites as well.

We had the best time making the mini-movies together. I played the role of cameraman and director while Alana was the 'talent.' Because we only have a small Sony Webbie HD video camera, we would first shoot the footage, with me being very careful not to get any scenes where Alana would be speaking directly into the camera. After shooting and editing the video, I'd then record a voice-over while Alana played a 'sound tract' on her keyboard to go along with the action in the film. We had a blast.

One of the movies we had the most fun doing was depicting Alana coming home from work after a long day at the office. I began shooting the video with her walking up the sidewalk while chatting on the cell phone until she reached the front door of our house. Once inside, I followed her with the camera into the bedroom where she removed her suit jacket then sat on the side of the bed to remove her heels, showing off her long legs. She then stood and pulled the blouse over her head then slipped her skirt over her rump and down her long legs onto the floor, leaving her standing in her bra and pantyhose. She sat back on the side of the bed and slowly ran her hands down her long legs to provocatively remove her pantyhose. She then reached for her robe and wrapped it around her as she walked into the shower where we continued filming.

Once we edited the film and got the shots we wanted, as always, Alana played the background music while I record the voiceover. I started with the phone conversation as she walked toward the door, "Yes, I did see him today. He's such a hottie, and I hear he has a big dick too (giggle giggle)." Once inside and taking off her shoes while sitting on the side of the bed I continued the voiceover with, "Oooo, my poor aching feet. I can't wait to get these shoes off and slip into something a little more comfortable." I continued with the oohs and ahhs as she ran her hands over her body while undressing. "That shower is going to feel ssoooo good, I can't wait to feel the warm water running all over my poor tired body," as she picked up her robe and walked into the bathroom.

It had been so much fun making that video and we decided to upload it on both of the dating sites. If I hadn't witnessed it, I would never have believed the results. On the 'geared to the transgender community' site she got a fair amount of attention. But, on the general public site, she got over 40,000 hits within a matter of a couple months. FORTY-THOUSAND. The number of 'hits' is an indication of how many people actually clicked to view her profile.

Back in the day when I was single I had set up a dating profile as well, on the SAME general public dating site. I doubt I got anywhere near 40 hits – but Alana got 40,000. It blew me away. The large number of hits reminded me of what Alan had said back in the day about swingers, the swinger clubs, the swinger magazines, etc. and that there wouldn't be such things if there weren't people who were interested in such things and willing to pay for such things. Swingers are there ... just like people who like transwomen are there – we're just not always aware they're there.

The information in Alana's profile and on the videos made it very clear she is a transwoman, and she even divulged in her profile that she had been diagnosed as HIV positive and STILL GOT 40,000 HITS. I gained a different understanding about swingers from the statement that if someone wasn't buying the magazines then they wouldn't be making enough money to continue to exist. I also gained a different understanding about the popularity of transwomen from the large number of hits Alana received on the dating site. If no one was interested in transwomen, then there would have been no hits on the profile – but there were 40,000. In both cases it taught me things aren't always what we think they are. I had no idea there were so many people in the swinger lifestyle, and I had no idea there were so many people into transwomen.

Although she wasn't contacted by 40,000 people, she did receive in excess of several hundred contacts, and they included both males and females. Of that number of contacts, she communicated with only a few but actually made friends with one man – George.

Alana and George exchanged email addresses and corresponded with one another over a period of several weeks. Then Alana asked if it would be OK to make arrangements to meet George in person and get to know him better. I agreed.

When we finally met George we both liked him. He was a few inches taller than Alana, slender muscular body, tan, dark hair, and brown eyes with a great 'country-boy' personality. Of course, the site where Alana and George made one another's acquaintance was a 'dating' site, and since Alan and I had had the multiple partner sexual experience together in the past, I agreed when Alana asked if the three of us could make a date to get together.

But, it wasn't just because we had shared the multiple partner experiences in the past that lead me to agreeing to our three-way date. It was also because, Alana, as a woman, is attracted to and has a desire to be with a man. That is one desire which I, personally, cannot fulfill. The desire Alana is experiencing is a natural physical desire ... the desire for a physical sexual experience between a man and a woman. And, again based solely on my own experiences, I understand sex can just be a satisfaction of physical desires.

George arrived and brought with him a bottle of our favorite wine. We had music playing and drank several glasses as the three of us enjoyed flirting with one another. Alana was totally female. I saw nothing but female. She looked female. She acted female. She looked small and submissive next to George. He was the only masculine energy in the room and was thoroughly enjoying his experience of being with two women. There was no question in my mind that George saw both of us as all-woman. I was somewhat surprised that I gained a sense of being 'happy' for Alana, the woman, grateful she had this opportunity to satisfy her desire of being with a man.

One thing I found quite surprising from being with George and experiencing his fully masculine energy was recognizing just how greatly the sexual energy between Alana and I has changed. I was consciously aware of my focus on the energy of the person, the feel of the body, but it wasn't until I experienced the masculine aggressive energy from George that I fully realized masculine energy absolutely no longer exists in Alana. I hadn't 'missed' the masculine energy because my focus was on the 'love' energy between the two of us. Having the experience of the masculine aggressive energy of George was good for both Alana and me.

When we were at our next appointment with Marcie, Alana's therapist, I felt I had to share with her the unexpected revelations, the feelings, the satisfaction I received from our shared experience with George. I wasn't really sure why I felt it was necessary to share this information with her, but, somehow I knew it was important information for her to know as a therapist.

I'm sure our openness and actions won't sit well with some folks, just like some of the information in Alana's book didn't sit well with everyone. However, I believe it is important to honestly share our feelings and experiences because I am aware of other cis-gender persons with a transgender spouse who have asked me questions about being faced with similar desires and feelings. I wouldn't dare suggest any married couple act upon their physical sexual desires ... either together or separately. However I would suggest each person in the relationship be willing to openly and honestly communicate with one another about their feelings and desires. I would also strongly recommend that each person takes time to hear the other and listen without judging anything said as 'right' or 'wrong.'

13

STATE OF CONFUSION

I remember as a teen living in the local housing projects walking into the kitchen in the middle of the night, flipping on the lights, and seeing roaches everywhere. Within seconds of the lights coming on, they scattered. As I continued to look around, soon there wasn't a roach one to be seen. I knew roaches existed, but, had never had any experience with roaches prior to that night. With a flip of a switch I learned they were everywhere and I learned in order to keep from being found out, they run and hide. But it was too late. I'd been made aware they were there, and being made aware of their existence made me feel uncomfortable.

Without having a better analogy, I find my experience with the transgender population can be somewhat like my roach experience. I've learned transgender people are everywhere, and quite often, they live life in hiding. And persons who are not transgender can feel uncomfortable when they are made aware someone is transgender.

My introduction to the majority of my transgender friends has been made through Facebook. My initial intention for establishing an "Alana's Spouse" Facebook account was to use it as a marketing tool for Alana's book. I quickly started getting friend requests from transgender individuals from not only other states, but other countries as well. Many times I've visited the page of the person making the friend request to learn more about that person, and find they have hundreds of friends who are also transgender. Although I sometimes find a friend or two in common on their page, there are usually only a few, which means I've just been made aware of the existence of many more transgender persons, and those numbers just keep on growing.

It is mind blowing to me the number of transgender persons who have crossed my life's path since that day in 2006 when I saw Alana for the first time. At that time, I was totally ignorant of transgender persons and had no idea the transgender population even existed, let alone knowing it is so large. My mind goes back to the statistic I found saying '1 out of every 100 people fall under the transgender umbrella,' and the census count indicating there are 315-MILLION people in the USA. If the statistics are anywhere near correct, that means 3-million-plus people in the USA are transgender. I'm not sure what the world population is, but believe it's really lots and lots of people. So I have to wonder what the number of transgender persons would be worldwide.

I live in the small rural town of Versailles, Kentucky with a population of approximately 8,000 people; therefore, 3-million-plus transgender people sounds like an extremely large number of people to me. With the possibility of such a large population of transgender people in the US, I wondered, "Where are they and why wasn't I made aware of their existence prior to 2006."

Then I had thoughts that caused me to look at the transgender population from a different perspective. If only 1 out of 100 people are transgender, then how many people can actually have any knowledge of the transgender experience? I figured the transperson has at least two other people who are familiar with their experience ... their parents. So that makes 3 out of 100 people who would have some level of knowledge about being transgender. Then I added the possibility of each transgender person at some point in time having a spouse and a child (like Alana did) – that brings my number of people aware of the transgender experience up to 5. Then I doubled that number to take into consideration other family members or friends who might be aware of the transgender person – like aunts, uncles, brothers, sisters, cousins. It's not a scientific formula, but it does give me a guesstimate there is a possibility that 10 out of 100, or only 10 percent, of the people alive on the earth at any given moment in time are somewhat aware of the transgender experience.

Of course, that also means 90 percent of the population of the USA, and the world, possibly could have absolutely no knowledge of the transgender experience what-so-ever ... which is exactly where I was prior to seeing Alana for the first time in 2006.

Then I thought that maybe I was unaware of transgender persons because I live in such a small town or that it is because I've spent all my life here in Kentucky. Alana talks about how she has been transgender all her life but didn't know what was 'wrong' with her until she learned about 'transgender' when she was in her mid-30's and discovered there was nothing 'wrong.' So, I figured living in Kentucky and not having access to information and resources was a contributing factor to our ignorance.

But then I watched the documentary, *"Becoming Chaz"* (on Netflix) and was surprised that someone who I'd think would have access to all the information and resources in the world, Chaz Bono, actually had very similar experiences as Alana when it came to not having the information that would explain what she/he was experiencing. (I use she/he here because of Chastity/Chaz). Chaz pointed out that he spent a lifetime struggling with his personal identity and was in his 40's before beginning his transition. Watching *"Becoming Chaz"* caused me to draw the conclusion that it's possible it doesn't matter your geographical location or economic status … especially if 90 percent of people are ignorant of the transgender experience.

If the transgender experience is unknown to 90 percent of the people in the world, then no wonder there is so much bigotry and fear when it comes to transgender individuals. The greatest fear any human faces is the fear of the unknown. I believe bigotry is often the result of ignorance … or a lack of knowledge of any experience. Because our greatest fear is the fear of the unknown, and the experience of being transgender is highly unknown, then we need to start making the experience known. Educating 90% of the world's population is a huge task … but it can be done by teaching one person at a time.

During the Civil Rights movement, as a child in the 1960's, I watched the news on our black and white TV screen from the safety of my little Kentucky town about the riots happening all over the country because of bigotry and discrimination toward persons of color. Seeing all that on TV was foreign to me and didn't mean much because I wasn't involved in the experiences happening across the nation. My child's mind couldn't understand 'hating' people simply because of the color of their skin. In my classroom there was just one black boy, and one black girl. They were my friends. I loved them just like I loved all of my other classmates. I couldn't get it in my head why all the violence shown on the TV was going on. It wasn't until I grew up that I realized the bigotry was a result, at least in part, because people were ignorant of and fearful of something they knew nothing about ... the experience of being born black.

It took the Civil Rights movement of the 60's to teach those who are not black that black people are just people ... nothing more and nothing less ... simply people. I totally agree with a statement made by leaders high in our National Government in 2013 that, "The transgender issue is the Civil Rights issue of our day." It's time to teach those who are ignorant of the transgender population – to teach 90 percent of the population of the United States, and the world – that transgender persons are 'just people' as well. It is through education and awareness that we eliminate the ignorance, and by making people aware of the transgender experience, it's no longer an 'unknown.' Therefore, we eliminate the fear of the unknown with knowledge, thereby giving us the ability to eliminate the bigotry, discrimination and most importantly, the hate crimes.

I've been thrown into the transgender community as an 'outsider looking in' through my relationship with Alana, and as such, I'm occasionally VERY CONFUSED, and find that it is often transgender persons who are actually *'in'* the community and make up the transgender population who cause much of my confusion.

In an effort to gain a better understanding of the transgender experience I've asked the same questions to many transgender individuals and find I get different answers and different viewpoints to those same questions much of the time – which can cause my confusion. It took me some time to realize the answer each individual gave is *their* understanding of *their* situation based on *their* own experiences as a transgender person. And each person's experience is different ... and that's true for all persons, transgender or not.

One area where I'm often confused is with terminology. I see and hear the words 'transgender' and 'transsexual' used interchangeably quite often. I've been in conversations with some people who would fight tooth and nail to their dying day trying to prove that the two words mean something different, yet, I've had similar conversations with others who refuse to let go of their concept that the two words mean the same thing. And it's true the two words can mean the same thing to some people while others believe they have very different definitions. Each person's 'definition' or 'understanding' of the words transgender and transsexual comes from within the person. Each person's understanding is 'correct' for that person ... although it may be 'incorrect' for others.

Personally, I understand the words as having different meaning based on my own experiences and the message conveyed to me by each word. I find many people prefer the word transsexual, however, personally, I prefer the word transgender.

For me, using the word transgender helps me understand better what I believe the trans experience to be since I do not actually have the experience of being trans. Because the word transgender contains 'trans,' as in transition, and 'gender' as having been born a male or female, I can easily understand transgender to mean a 'transition of gender.'

The word transsexual causes my brain to go into a state of confusion because I can't get my mind wrapped around the 'sexual' part of the word. Again, I understand the 'trans' part to mean transition, but my confusion with the 'sexual' part comes from MY understanding the word 'sex' to mean a physical act. From my understanding, the word sex does not convey gender. Male and female are gender distinctions in my brain. I believe anyone can have sex and that encompasses straight, gay, bi, lesbian, and everything from one extreme to the other (and apparently many Americans believe the act of sex can be performed with a cigar). Therefore when I see or hear the word transsexual, it confuses me as to what type of 'sex' is being 'transitioned.' It's as if my mind goes into overload with questions. Is it the person's sexual preference that's changing? Is the same gender sexual preference changing or is it the opposite gender sexual preference being transitioned? Is the transsexual making a transition to/from straight, gay, lesbian, or bi sex?" The word transsexual just doesn't convey any clear understanding for me ... it only causes me confusion. I just can't get a clear concept from the word transsexual like I can with the word transgender. So, whenever I see or hear the word transsexual, in my mind I say, *"oh, to me that word means how I understand the word transgender."* I would never try to change the words anyone uses; I only try to gain understanding of their words ... and I can do that only through my own brain filters.

I remember telling some new friends about being married to a transgender person and one of them said, "Oh, you mean a chick-with-a-dick." I'd never heard that term before, but, it conveyed to me an understanding I'd never considered before of the person I married ... a 'chick' who has a dick. I'd had a relationship with the dick long before I began a relationship with the chick, so I could understand what I believe Alana's experience to be when it was put that way. I had also gained understanding that "some women are born with a penis" from what Valerie Spencer said in the movie, *"Beautiful Daughters."*

I've also learned that using certain words can totally piss some people off, while other people actually embrace those very same words. Of course, how someone feels about any word depends on the understanding conveyed to that individual by that word based on their own personal experiences and definition ... like the words transgender and transsexual does for me. Words are not 'right' or 'wrong' for every person ... words simply convey meaning and that meaning can be different based on who is saying or hearing the word.

I believe no one should use words to deliberately hurt another person. I don't particularly like the word Bitch when some people use that term to describe me, but I've been called a bitch more than once in my life when the person using the word is doing so to try to offend me. Yet, based on my own definition of the word Bitch, there are times when I 'wear it proudly' ... to me a bitch is often used to depict a woman who is independent, strong, proud, aggressive, and successful. Yep, there can be times when I wouldn't mind being called a bitch.

She-male is one of those words I've learned since becoming an 'outsider looking in' member of the transgender population that can really make many transwoman ready to fight. Like hearing 'chick with a dick' conveyed some sort of understanding I hadn't had prior to hearing the term, 'she-male' helped me with gaining an understanding of how 'Alan' was really 'Alana' ... it helped me envision Alana as being a 'she' who had been born with 'male' parts (and, again, related to Valarie Spencer's comment ... at least in my mind).

I personally know some transwomen who are OK with and even embrace the term she-male being used when attempting to educate about their particular transgender experience. Although they identify as female, they still maintain a great relationship with their penis and do not allow having a penis to be the determining factor for gender ... therefore, in agreement with my understanding of the word, they are 'she' with 'male' parts. Yet, I've heard some of these same transwomen say they would never admit to another trans person their acceptance of the term 'she-male' because it is generally seen as such a derogatory term in the overall trans population.

I've seen several books, resources, even websites that offer a 'glossary of terms' where the same word is defined differently from one place to another. Occasionally the difference is ever so slight, but sometimes I find them totally contradictory of one another. And, on top of the different definitions for a single word, the word itself often changes. For example, at the first transgender support group I attended with Alana I was told I was a GG, or genetic girl. However, I used that term in a Facebook post and was reprimanded for using an 'out of date' term. I had just learned the term ... I'm totally new to the transgender population, and I'm getting reprimanded for not knowing what someone considers to be the 'proper' term. The person commenting on my post in a 'not so nice' manner explained that today's term is 'cis.' I looked up the word 'cis' and found it derives from a scientific origin and although I could understand how 'cis' was being used in relation to GG, I better understand and can easily explain the meaning of GG, but I found 'cis' to be somewhat more complicated and difficult for me to explain.

Every person should have the freedom to use whatever word works best for them without another person saying that word is 'incorrect' ... ever hear, "one man's trash is another man's treasure." The acceptance or rejection of a term comes from the perspective of the individual based on their experience with and understanding of that term ... which brings us right back to 'each experience is different.'

I do have a favorite term I've learned in relation to transgender persons ... that is 'genderqueer' as I understand the definition to be 'neither male nor female but an androgynous hybrid of both or a rejection of both.' I like that word and definition because to me it gives each person the freedom to be as they choose to be ... either both genders or neither. Also, I can justify in my mind every person alive as 'genderqueer' to some degree because each person has both "X" and "Y" chromosomes, or some level of both 'testosterone' and 'estrogen' hormones in their bodies ... but chromosomes and hormones are scientific explanations which I know nothing about. So I just think of it as everyone having both 'male traits' and 'female traits' which, in my brain at least, explains how we are all genderqueer to some degree.

One person who comes to mind whenever I think of my perfect example of genderqueer is the Art Ist D (theartistd.com) ... a radio personality Alana and I had the great fortune of becoming acquainted with several months ago. D publically expresses sometimes as male, and sometimes as female ... an ability I greatly admire and believe is far above and beyond FABULOUS.

I recently watched a YouTube video where Howard Stern interviewed Buck Angel and continued to try to use the word 'woman' to classify Buck based on the condition that he has a vagina while, at the same time, Buck continued to use the word 'man.' They voiced their respective opinions back and forth a time or two as to why the word they each choose to use was the 'correct' word. Finally Buck said something like, "We could argue over this until we both die."

Of course each, from their own personal perspective, was correct in what they were saying based on their own experiences and understanding. Howard's understanding of what a male should be is someone born with a penis and what a female should be is someone born with a vagina. Information he's been given his entire life and information the majority of society believes as truth. The concept of a male with a vagina was simply foreign to Howard because he's not had the experience of being a man born with a vagina. Howard's understanding came from the information he has been given all his life and the new information that a man can have a vagina was simply a concept that was not his 'truth.'

However, Buck was correct in saying he is a man because he knows, from personal experience, that a man can be born with a vagina and it is NOT the sex organ that determines gender. Actually, Buck used a term I'd never heard before ... mangina ... but I bet we will be hearing the term mangina more and more as time goes by and society becomes educated on transmen.

There was a time in my life when I would have said Howard was 100% correct because I had received the same information during my 50+ years of life that Howard had been given ... that men are born with a penis and women are born with a vagina. However, from my personal experience with Alana and other persons in the transgender population, I have learned that in actuality it is Buck who is correct. I have learned that 'most' men are born with a penis and 'most' women are born with a vagina, however, 'some' women are born with a penis and 'some' men are born with a vagina. Again, just like those folks back in the day who believed the earth was flat, it took the experience of someone else to teach them that they were incorrect in their belief ... it took the experience of someone else to teach them that things are different from what they had been taught all their lives and had come to believe ... that the earth actually is round. Transpersons are proving that the belief that all men are born with a penis and all women are born with a vagina is a false belief. A penis or a vagina is not the determining factor for gender.

****

My real education regarding trans persons began with attending the 2012 Southern Comfort Conference in Atlanta, Georgia. Although I'd made a few transgender friends on Facebook, I'd gained most of my understanding of the transgender experience from being around Alana, whose desire it is to transition from male to female. So, I thought that was what being transgender meant, wanting to transition from one gender to the other. But I quickly learned being transgender means so much more than just feeling like you were born in the body of one gender while identifying as another. Although, that can be a proper explanation of the transgender experience, I've learned there is not just ONE WAY to be transgender.

One afternoon while at SCC I was sitting next to Alana as she had been chatting with one of the other attendees, Becky, and for whatever reason, she left the two of us alone for a short period of time. One of the questions I had heard several of the SCC attendees often asking one another was, "Do you present en-fem full-time?" So, I thought that asking this question would be a good way for me to break the ice and start a conversation with Becky, so I looked at her and said, "Do you present en-fem full time?"

Without hesitation she almost yelled, "Hell no, and I wouldn't want to either. I enjoy being Eric as much as I enjoy being Becky."

I immediately envisioned the robot from *"Lost in Space"* flailing his arms and shouting, "warning, warning Will Robinson." My mind was blown as I thought *"does not compute, does not compute. How can you be transgender if you like being BOTH male and female?"*

"But I thought being transgender meant wanting to transition from one gender to another." I said with a totally confused look on my face.

Becky said, "For some it does, but not for everyone who identifies as fitting under the trans umbrella. I identify as being transgender, but, I don't want to live my entire life in female form, just like I don't want to live my entire life in male form either. I enjoy being both. Of course, my opportunities to be female are somewhat limited, but, when I'm given the chance, I love being a woman."

"Then are you a crossdresser?" I asked the question because crossdresser was another term I'd heard since being introduced to the trans population.

"Some people believe a crossdresser fits under the trans umbrella, and some do not." Becky answered. "I believe most people think of a crossdresser as someone who enjoys occasionally dressing in the clothing of the opposite gender but not necessarily with the desire to live their life presented in a gender other than the one in which they were born. At least, that's what crossdresser means to me."

"Then I don't understand. You just said your understanding of a crossdresser is someone who enjoys occasionally dressing in the clothing of the opposite gender. Didn't you just tell me that you like being a man, but you like dressing as a female, you just don't want to do it all the time? I'm confused. How are you trans if you don't have the desire to change genders?"

"I identify as a transgender person because I'm not just 'putting on the clothes' of different genders, I'm expressing and experiencing my life in different genders. I enjoy being male and I enjoy being female."

"Why do you sometimes say 'trans' and sometimes say 'transgender?' Is there a difference in the two words, or is trans just short for transgender?"

"Technically, transgender is a sub-category of sorts under the trans umbrella. Think of a big umbrella over a lot of people and those people can be put into various sub-categories that have names like crossdresser, transgender, transsexual, gender queer, intersex, and other ways of fitting into the trans population. These are just a very few of the sub-categories you might find under the trans umbrella. There can be debate in the trans community itself as to which sub-categories should go under the umbrella and which should not. Each sub-category, although perceived as different, may contain some similarities to other categories; yet, they all fit under the umbrella or into the overall trans community. And sometimes one person can identify as fitting into more than one sub-category.

Often in print you'll see the word trans followed by an asterisk (trans*) to represent the umbrella because so much fits under that umbrella. I would be impossible to list every situation that would fit under the trans umbrella, and not everyone is in agreement as to what should be under the umbrella, so using the asterisk allows each person to interpret the word trans to encompass whatever understanding they associate with the word."

"Another lesson learned," I thought. My only knowledge of being transgender had come from my experience with Alana. My conversation with Becky made me realize Alana's experience is by no means the 'blueprint' for the way all trans persons should be. Not having the experience of being trans myself, I just thought what I'd learned from Alana was the way all trans persons are.

Later that evening I went to listen to the Karaoke singers while Alana chatted in the bar with some new-found friends. A beautiful young transwoman came into the crowded area where I was and began looking around for an empty seat. I spoke to her and said, "You're welcome to sit with me if you'd like."

She took me up on my invitation and sat at my table. I wanted to start a conversation to help us both feel more at ease, but, wasn't sure I should ask the 'do you get to present en-fem full-time' question after my experience with Becky. So I just said, "How are you doing, hun?"

She was beautiful, tall, blond, and maybe in her early 30's. I guess I give off an air of 'you are safe and can say anything to me' because, as many people have done with me often, she opened up and said, "I'm confused."

"Me too," I chuckled, but without explaining my confusion, I asked, "What are you confused about?"

"I need to decide if I want to be a man or a woman."

"Funny you should say that, because I was chatting with one of the conference attendees earlier who said they like being both."

Her face lit up as she very expressively said, "I DO TOO," seemingly happy that someone other than herself liked the ability to express both genders.

"Then why don't you just be both?" I questioned.

"Well, we don't live in a society that allows for that, now do we," she retorted as if I had asked a ridiculous question. "Society forces us to make a choice, which is really hard on me since I identify as both genders and feel comfortable as either."

"So, you're saying that in order to be what 'society' thinks you should be, you're willing to give up a portion of yourself ... one gender or the other ... just to please 'society' instead of living your life expressing both genders to please yourself."

"Of course," she answered sounding as if there was no choice other than to do as society demanded.

Her words made me think of how some trans persons had told Alana she 'couldn't possibly be transgender' because she hasn't had any surgeries and doesn't always wear dresses. Yet, Alana explained she is always 'Alana,' had always been Alana even during those years she struggled to hide herself and will always BE Alana no matter what clothes she's wearing or even when she's not wearing any clothes. Alana hadn't changed being herself just because of how others thought she should be. Yet, this young person was telling me she was confused because she felt like she had to change somehow to live her life as one gender or the other based on what 'society' or 'others' were demanding.

"Honey, it's your life. You get to make all the decisions having to do with your life. You can make those decisions influenced by society if that's what you choose to do, but it's not society that ultimately lives your life … it's you. Personally, I feel like you might have the best of both worlds. There's no way I could get away with living as two genders, but, apparently you can. Why do you think you must make the decision on how to live your life based on what society dictates?"

"Because that's the way it is for all of us. We have to live our lives in a manner that society accepts," she said in a matter-of-fact tone.

I didn't say more because all of a sudden I felt sad for this beautiful young person who had the whole world at their feet with the ability to be anything, but she didn't see the situation that way. I saw someone in a gifted position of being able to live life as they pleased. I saw someone in the position of having access to opportunities most people, those limited to the experience of living life as only one gender, could never have ... opportunities of knowing what it's like to be a man ... and a woman ... or to choose either at their own discretion. But, she saw her life as being one riddled with confusion and difficult decisions because she believed she had to give up some part of self in order to please 'society.'

It wasn't long before a handsome young man approached and asked her if he could buy her a drink. "Here," I said, offering him my seat. "I was just getting ready to leave."

He thanked me for my seat and I walked away.

****

Alana and I chose a seat at a table with other conference attendees to have our dinner in the dining room. Everyone at the table said their hello's then started polite conversations with the person seated next to them as we all ate our meal. Directly across from me were two transwomen who were carrying on a conversation together, and, because of where I was seated, I could hear every word of their conversation. It went like this:

    Lady 1:   Hi, my name is Linda.
    Lady 2:   Hi Linda, I'm Sue.
    Lady 1:   Hi Sue. Where are you from?
    Lady 2:   I live in France. How about you? Are you from the states?
    Lady 1:   Yes, I live right here in Atlanta actually.

Do you get to present en-fem full-time? (*"see, there's that question again,"* I thought.)
 Lady 2: No
 Lady 1: Oh, I see. Are you married?
 Lady 2: Yes, and you?
 Lady 1: Well, I was, but my wife died two years ago. She had cancer. I'm just thankful she didn't suffer long like some cancer patients do. So, have you been going to transgender conferences very long?
 Lady 2: Yes, close to 30 years now. And you?
 Lady 1: When my wife was alive I couldn't do anything like this. But this is my second year for attending SCC.
 Lady 2: So, you never told your wife?
 Lady 1: No, I just couldn't. Have you told your wife?
 Lady 2: No, I just can't bring myself to tell her. I'm afraid she wouldn't understand and I'd never do anything that might cause me to lose her.
 Lady 1: So, how long have you been married?
 Lady 2: 30 years.

My heart broke. I just wanted to hug both these women and tell them what beautiful strong spirits they are. I had to fight hard to hold back my tears which made eating my meal difficult. I tried to contemplate what it might be like to feel you must hide who you are from everyone in your life … to hide yourself from someone as close as your spouse … and do so for your entire lifetime together. I couldn't comprehend living life in such a manner. I hurt not only for the two people in front of me who had been living their lives in secret, but for their wives as well and the countless others who have experienced such lives.

****

"You're in for a total mind fuck," are the words Trudy had said to me my first day at the SCC conference. She was right as long as I tried to 'figure it all out' within my own mind ... as long as I tried to conjure up some sort of understanding for **ME**.

For example, one of the things that would cause me confusion while at the SCC is when I'd be in the bar and I'd see men flirting with and buying drinks for the transgender women. My brain would try to figure out just what it was I was seeing as I'd think, *"ok, so that 'woman' was born as a 'man' and is being hit on by a 'man,' so, am I seeing a gay situation?"* Then I'd think, *"Wait a minute Bobbie, you're doing what so many others do when you tell them about being married to Alana. You're trying to categorize everything based on YOUR level of experience and understanding. Just accept what you actually 'see' – a man flirting with a woman, and let it go at that. Stop trying to explain everything and just accept what is ... let it be."* I'm not saying I ever reached a level of understanding anything, but I did reach a level of accepting things without it being necessary to understand or figure out how things came to be.

Another example of confusion for me was when I was dancing with a transgender woman on the final night of the conference who told me she worked at a gay bar. During our conversation she said she was occasionally 'hit on by gay men' and that upset her. She said, "can't they understand I'm straight."

I was dancing with a transwoman, and from my understanding based on what Alana and others have explained to me, a transwoman identifies as a woman, therefore, the prefix of trans is just a way to describe that this woman had to undergo some aspect of transitioned to be a woman ... and that transition can include anything from putting on lipstick to having gender surgery. So, from my perspective based on what I'd learned about transwomen, the person I was dancing with was a woman. Yet, 'she' just told me she identifies as 'straight' because 'she' is attracted to 'women.'

"I'm so confused," I thought because initially my brain wanted to figure things out. *"Doesn't this 'woman' dancing with me who had been born in a 'male' body have to be speaking from a male perspective if she is describing herself as 'straight'? How is it possible for this transwoman, who is attracted to women, describe herself as straight unless this transwoman still identifies as male? If this person I'm dancing with is presenting as female and is attracted to females, then how can this person identify as straight ... wouldn't she be a lesbian?"*

My head began to spin as I tried to figure out what I'd just heard. I quickly thought, *"This is apparently another one of those mind fuck situations Trudy tried to warn me about."* Again I decided to give up trying to figure things out based on my level of understanding and simply take what she had said as truth ... her truth, based on her experiences, perspectives, and understanding. I didn't have to figure out her truth in order to understand she was speaking truth, and her truth was that she is a 'transwoman' attracted to 'women' who identifies as 'straight.'

My HUSBAND Looks Better in Lingerie Than I Do ... DAMN IT

****

My state of confusion wasn't limited to our participation in the 2012 Southern Comfort Conference. One afternoon I was in a local government office on personal business and ran into a friend I'd graduated from high school with. She asked me how things were going with Alana's book and I began talking about some of the experiences I'd had at SCC.

After talking for a few minutes, I saw my friend's boss come from her office, cross her arms, and stand a couple feet behind my friend as she stared intently at me while I spoke. *"Oops, you've worn out your welcome here Bobbie," I thought to myself. "I don't think this conversation is going over very well with the boss lady. I think you're about to be asked to leave."*

Then I said, "Well, I guess I'd better quit talking and let you get back to work." I turned to leave, and sure enough, the boss lady said, "Excuse me, will you come into my office for a moment."

In my head I'm already playing out the scenario of conflict I expect to happen when she looked at me and said, "I'm so glad to hear you talking about your experience of attending the Southern Comfort Conference. You see, I have a transgender child ... female-to-male. It's rare to get to meet someone else who has a transgender person in their family ... especially here in Versailles."

It definitely was NOT what I had expected to hear. She shared with me that her child had come out as a male in high school and recently graduated. She showed me his picture ... a proud mama showing off her son's picture. She went on to explain that although he was doing seemingly well with his transition, it was she and her husband who were in need of education and support.

I asked if she was familiar with PFLAG and she said although she was familiar with the organization, her son didn't identify as 'one of them' (words her son used) and would not attend transgender support groups of any kind, and would get quite upset when she and her husband expressed wanting to attend transgender related functions. She explained that her son had expressed that when his parents attended such groups he took it as a 'slap in the face' as an acknowledgement that he had been born 'different.'

She explained that, from her child's perspective, he had always been a 'male,' he did not identify as having been born in the 'wrong' body because he did not understand his body as the determining factor in him being a male. In his mind, he had been born a boy and would always be a boy regardless of body parts and to attend anything transgender related would be improper for him.

I was confused again. I had grown to understand that a transman identifies as a man and that a transwoman identifies as a woman, but I couldn't wrap my mind around a male born in the body of a female having no concept of being trans. Again I decided to simply hear what was being said and accept that 'a male born in a female body can have no concept of being trans' and allow the truth of the person to simply 'be.'

Some months later Alana and I were at a local LOVEboldly (www.loveboldly.net) meeting: an organization whose focus is to provide a safe place to discuss faith and sexuality. There was another transwoman in attendance and she made the statement, "Why would I want to go to a gay bar? Gay bars are places where persons who are attracted to the same gender go to meet one another. I'm a woman. I'm interested in men who want a woman ... straight men ... you don't find straight men in gay bars." That was another concept or perspective I would never have thought of on my own. Although this woman openly identifies as a transwoman (even to the point of saying one of her favorite tops has the word 'TRANS-tastic' that fits across her quite large breasts), she first and foremost identifies as a 'woman' who is interested in a 'straight' relationship. Again I decided that, although hers was a perspective and understanding I'd never thought of, it was 'her' truth. Again I decided to simply allow what I understood her words to 'be' ... she is a woman interested in a relationship with a man.

For the longest time I spent much of my life living in a state of confusion because I believed everything had to somehow fit into MY way of understanding of how things 'should' be. But I've come to learn that my understanding of what is 'right' or 'wrong' is simply that ... MY understanding. What is 'right' or 'wrong' for me is 'right' or 'wrong' for ONLY me. I, nor anyone, can tell someone else what should or should not be right or wrong for any person other than myself. Every decision of right or wrong comes from the individual making that decision based on their experiences and perspectives. Right or wrong can be different for each person.

I've learned that some transwomen identify as straight even though they are attracted to women ... they don't have to identify as lesbian just because I thought they were supposed to. I've learned that some guys born with female parts identify as guys and do not consider themselves transgender, even though I thought if a guy was born with female parts then they had to call themselves trans. I've learned that some transwomen, who are proud of being trans, can have a straight relationship ... even though I thought that if the transwoman had been born in a male body then they couldn't experience a straight relationship. I've learned that by allowing without needing to figure everything out in order to fit **MY** understanding, I eliminated my state of confusion situation. I learned to just LET IT BE.

I've learned that transgender people are just people who, like every other person I know, want to live their life in peace ... who want to enjoy a loving relationship with another person ... who want to have a job that allows them to provide for themselves and their family ... who want to be treated with the same respect as any other person would be. I've learned that no matter what the person's life journey, people are just people.

14

MORE THAN TWO SIDES TO THIS COIN

A speech I heard at the Southern Comfort Conference sticks in my mind. The transwoman was talking about various issues faced by transgender persons specifically, including various areas of discrimination ... such as health care coverage, employment issues, etc. She urged transpersons to make themselves known in their families, in their neighborhoods, and especially in their work places. She explained how living stealth could be detrimental to the trans population striving to achieve equality. (My understanding of the word stealth means to live life in the gender in which one has transitioned into without making it known they underwent a transition to live as that gender.)

What she said made perfect sense to me. I thought of her speech as a, "Be trans, be loud, and be proud" pep talk. It made me want to yell, "Hell yeah."

After all, I was in my 50's before I was made aware of the trans population. Her question, "How can the trans population ever achieve equality if they remain in hiding?" made perfect sense to me. Yet, that's exactly where the majority of the trans persons I've met so far live ... in hiding. I know so many transgender persons who only present their true selves in situations that allow them to do so safely. I know so many trans persons who go to work every day as the person the world expects them to be instead of the person they really are only to return to their homes, alone, where it is safe for them to slip into something that allows them to be themselves for a few hours before they must go back to being who others think they should.

One experience in particular that comes to mind has to do with a person Alana met online ... Gina. They quickly became friends and Gina expressed wanting to learn more about applying cosmetics and dressing, so Alana invited her over. Alana (presenting en-fem) answered the door and Gina (in male form) stepped into the foyer. She and Alana exchanged their hellos and I came from the other room to greet our guest. Although Alana had told her she is married, Gina was obviously taken aback when she saw me come into the room. I thought she was going to turn around and run back out the door. She quickly said to Alana, "I didn't know anyone else would be here." I could tell she was extremely uncomfortable.

I extended my hand and said, "Hi Hun, I'm Bobbie, Alana's spouse." She acted as if she didn't know whether she should shake my hand or make some excuse to leave. With a 'deer caught in the headlight' expression she'd look at Alana, then back at me, then back to Alana, then back at me. Finally after several seconds of hesitation she took my hand and said, "Hi I'm XXX, giving a male name."

I smiled and patted the back of her hand as she shook mine and said, "I've only heard Alana refer to you as Gina ... is it OK if I call you Gina as well."

She raised her eyebrows as if surprised and said, "Sure."

We offered her a seat and chatted for a few minutes to become better acquainted and allow Gina to become more comfortable with her surroundings. Finally Alana said, "So, did you bring some outfits like we discussed." Gina quickly looked at Alana with a surprised look on her face, nodded her head in my direction, and asked, "You mean it's OK with *her* here?"

Alana laughed and said, "Yes, Bobbie is going to help with your makeup and help accessorize the outfits."

Reluctantly Gina stood and headed out the door toward her vehicle. I didn't know if she'd just get in her car and drive away or choose to come back into the house with the outfits. After some length of time she came back to the front door with two pieces of luggage in tow.

I said, "Do you want to do your makeup before we start dressing." Again Gina was initially hesitant when I began to help her with the cosmetics. However, it didn't take long for her to realize she was in a safe place and started to relax a bit.

After the makeup session Gina went into our extra bedroom where Alana had put her luggage and came out in one of the outfits she'd brought with her. We tried various different jewelry pieces to accent the outfit. Once she was all dolled up she asked if it were OK for her to wear the outfit for a bit while we talked. We three ladies sat and chatted while we enjoyed a glass of wine and Gina and Alana smoked a couple cigarettes.

I asked Gina if I could take her picture with our digital camera and she said, "Only if you promise me you will delete it afterword." I promised, took her picture, and showed it to her.

She stood staring at the picture on the camera for a moment before saying, "I've never had a picture taken of me in female mode before. Except for what I see in the mirror, I've never seen myself dressed as a female." Then she smiled real big and said, "I kinda like the way I look."

I smiled back and said, "Why don't you model some of your outfits and we'll do a photo session?" For the next couple hours Gina would change from one outfit into another and strike various poses as I took her picture. Initially the poses were rather rigid, but after a short time, and a second glass of wine, she got more and more animated with her poses. She was having the best time … and so were we.

After a while she asked if it were OK for her to shower to remove the makeup and any traces of being fem to return to male form … the form in which she must live her life. She and I stood together and I let her delete all the pictures we had taken from the camera. She would take a second or two to view each picture prior to deleting it and said, "I hate having to delete these but I can't take a chance on them getting out." After deleting the last picture she handed me the camera back. Our fun day had ended.

Once back in male mode, packed, and ready to go Gina hugged both me and Alana and said, "You have no idea what this day has meant to me. You are the only people on earth who have EVER seen me, Gina, as who

I am. You see, my wife doesn't know. I have an executive position in a well-known company and have often attended conferences solely for the opportunity to dress en-fem. I've sat alone in hotel rooms for an entire week at a time during several conferences just to be me. I've never been able to share who I am with anyone else in my life. Thank you so very much for this day ... it means the world to me."

And it meant so much to Alana and me that something as insignificant as helping someone apply makeup and taking a few pictures made her feel so good.

****

I've learned another side of this multi-faceted coin has to do with 'outing' someone. Unfortunately I've felt the heartbreaking pain of unintentionally outing a friend. It was at the Lexington Pride Festival where Alana had her first book signing. My son had come by in support of Alana and a friend of ours who has completed transition came by about the same time.

Of course, I introduced my son and our friend, but during the introduction I said, "This is the person Terry told us she went to school with." Without realizing what I had done, I had outed my transgender friend by explaining their connection with Terry. He immediately gave me a disgusted look and walked away. I hadn't realized I'd done something bad, so I had no idea why my friend had walked away, nor did I understand why I didn't hear from him over the next several months.

Finally I contacted him personally and said, "I want to apologize to you. I know I've done something wrong in order for you to be so angry with me, but I don't know what I've done." He accepted my apology and proceeded to explain to me that by identifying him as 'the person Terry went to school with' and knowing that during those school days he had not accomplished transition, then I had outed him as a transperson. He explained that some people do not want to be associated with their past and often that comes from wanting to escape the memories of bad experiences lived during that time because of being unable to be themselves.

With his explanation I had been made aware of two sides of the transgender coin ... why it is important to some to live openly as a transgender person ... and why it is important to some to live in stealth.

Although I can understand the reasons for some persons to live in stealth, and believe that is their decision not someone else's to make, I can't help but admire those persons who are openly trans who desire to bring attention to the transgender population ... like Chaz Bono, Buck Angel, Janet Mock, and Dr. Marcie Bowers just to name a few.

A couple years before meeting Dr. Bowers at the 2012 SCC, Alana and I watched a documentary that shared the details of Dr. Bower's transition and medical practice. After meeting Dr. Bowers I shared a FB post something to the effect of, "We were so excited to meet Dr. Marcie Bowers, a transgender male-to-female, ..." Within minutes of making that post I had several transgender persons reprimand me for pointing out the fact that Dr. Bowers had transitioned and accused me of outing her. Again, I couldn't understand what I had done wrong, especially since Dr. Bowers herself had told the world she is a male-to-female transwoman via her documentary.

I've met transpersons who live stealth, like my friend I introduced my son to at the Pride Fest. I've met transpersons who live in hiding, like the ladies who sat across the table from us at dinner that evening whose conversation I overheard ... and Gina. And, I've met transpersons who live life out loud. Each person has their own reasons for living life as they choose to live it. I can understand how some want to live stealth. It breaks my heart to think that some must live in hiding. And I love it when I can share the experiences of transpersons who choose to live their lives loud and proud. But, most of all, I am extremely thankful to be in a situation where I can shout it from the rooftops, "My spouse is transgender."

In November 2013 Alana had the privilege of being the speaker during the Transgender Day of Remembrance event held at Transylvania University in Lexington, KY. I sat in the room filled with LGBT college students, their friends, families, and supporters of the LGBT community. I so very much admired the young people for simply and openly being themselves. There was very much a 'this is who and what I am and that's the way it is' atmosphere in the room. No one seemed to feel the necessity to hide who they are. Everyone accepted each person in the room regardless of their uniqueness and individuality. It was a beautiful experience. Each person just 'be-ing' and each person just 'let it be.'

15

IT'S REALLY ALL THE SAME

I remember as a kid in grades 1 through 8 in Burgin, KY, a town even smaller than the one we live in now, my exposure to diversity was by having one black girl and one black guy in the same class at school. I attended Burgin school from 1960 through 1968. During that time we watched the Civil Rights happenings on our black and white TV set at home. I was so far removed from all the turmoil we saw on TV and couldn't understand what was going on because the only black people I knew were just kids in my class who were exactly like everyone else except for the color of their skin. I wasn't aware that because of that one difference, having a skin color other than the skin color I have, they could be denied certain rights and freedoms that are mine. I didn't understand prejudice. I had no life experiences that caused me to know prejudice.

By the time I divorced my first husband in the mid 1990's I had been taught through life experiences that we are all different. Society had taught me that some ethnicities are 'supposed' to be better than others. That was the time when I met a very handsome Mexican man who worked on one of the local horse farms. He couldn't speak English, and I couldn't speak Spanish, but we started dating. Some folks frowned on our relationship asking, "What will the neighbors say about you dating a Mexican man." Others asked, "Why would you waste your time dating someone who has a lowly job of working on a horse farm." My answer was, "As soon as the neighbors start making my house payments, then I might be concerned with what they have to say about me, otherwise, who gives a rat's ass what the neighbors say. My neighbors don't live my life, I do. And as for the working on the horse farms, my first husband of 22 years worked on a horse farm and no one seemed to have a problem with it."

"Yes, but he was white. Being Mexican is different," they would say.

"How is it different?" I'd ask and they'd say, "It just is."

"Why?" I'd ask and they'd say, "It just is."

Although there were no answers to my questions of how and why, I knew that it was true my neighbors might look down on me in some manner because I chose to date someone 'different.'

Soon, the thought of 'difference' began to intrigue me. I thought, *"If we're so different, this Mexican man and me, then maybe it will be fun to learn firsthand just what those differences are. Once I've spent time with this 'different' person, then maybe I will be able to answer my own questions of how and why from having the experience of being with him."* I began feeling excited about being in the position to learn how we are so different. Then, if someone ever asked me how we are different or why we are different I'd be able to give them a definitive answer instead of just saying, "It just is." I looked forward to learning something new ... learning what was so different between us.

We went on a few dates, and for the life of me, I couldn't tell how dating this man was any different from dating anyone else I'd ever gone out with. When we'd go out to dinner he'd open the car door for me, he'd open the door at the restaurant for me, he'd choose his meal from the menu just like everyone else, he'd enjoy having a beer like anyone else, he'd cut up his steak and chew his food just like anyone else. It all seemed the same to me. I couldn't wait to learn something 'different.'

Then we made plans for us to spend our first night together. *"OK,"* I thought, *"going out in public is one thing, but being at home behind closed doors is not like being out in public. Maybe tonight is when I get a glimpse of how we are so different."* That night we had sex, the SAME way I'd ever had sex with anyone else before. Nothing different there. The next morning he showered. He washed his hair with shampoo and used soap to wash his body. Nothing different yet. He brushed his teeth with a toothbrush and toothpaste. Still nothing different. He even combed his hair with a comb, and shaved his beard with a razor. I began feeling disappointed because I wanted to learn firsthand about the differences everyone insisted existed. I kept waiting for something different to take place, but it never did. Instead of learning what our differences are, what I did learn was just how much alike we are, and that society's teaching of 'difference' is false.

Then in 2006 I saw Alana for the first time ... the man I had known as Alan for nearly 30-years presenting as a woman. Initially I thought, *"Now that's different, even freaky, and I don't want to have anything to do with something so different."* However, as time passed I learned the person is the same person I'd always known. I learned 'the lips are the same lips, the arms are the same arms, etc.' But I thought it was all supposed to be 'unacceptable' because being transgender is so different – I thought being transgender was supposed to be something bizarre. Yet from having a personal experience with someone transgender ... something I'd been told all my life was insane, freaky, different ... I learned everything was really the same. Again, I learned 'difference' was a false teaching.

A year or so after Alana and I were married a friend loaned us a CD of a TV show called, *"Queer as Folk."* Initially I was a little uncomfortable watching the scenes of intimacy between same gender couples. I had been taught all my life that intimacy and love between same gender couples was different and, therefore, wrong. As I watched the show I quickly learned, once again, the feelings between the same gender partners are the same feelings as any I've had in my various relationships. Again I learned about the similarities every couple shares instead of confirmation in a belief in difference.

There was one particular scene that really spoke to me. The mother of one of the gay men began a straight relationship with a man. Her boyfriend came into the diner where the mother worked as a waitress. Her son and several of his gay friends had gathered in the diner. As the boyfriend entered the diner he approached the mother/waitress and gave her a kiss. One of the gay men said, "Well, look at that, they do it the same way we do." I found it quite profound that the 'they do it like us' observation came from the perspective of a gay person viewing a straight couple because from my perspective, a straight person viewing a gay couple, I had never before considered a same gender relationship could be 'the same way we do.'

I'm not sure what I had expected the interaction between a same gender couple to be, but, I believed all my life 'they' were 'different' although no one had ever been able to explain to me how or why. Just like I'd been taught persons with a skin color other than mine are different, just like I had been taught persons speaking a language other than English are different, I had been taught that persons who are gay, lesbian, bi, or transgender are different. I've come to know that ALL these teaching are false teachings. We are all the same.

16

WHY IN THE WORLD

Without exception, EVERY transgender person I've met or have become acquainted with, and there have been thousands at this point, are ordinary people desiring the same things as every other person I've ever met ... be safe from harm, share the love of a spouse/family/friends, have a roof over their heads, clothes on their back, food in their stomach, earn a sustainable income ... in other words, to simply LIVE LIFE.

Yet, at the same time, EACH transgender person I've met or have become acquainted with has been EXTRAORDINARY in regard to what it takes to be themselves. Personally, I cannot imagine the experience of being transgender. It must take an extremely strong spirit to endure such a life experience.

On several occasions I've had transgender friends share with me their pain from loss of family. Having your parents disown you is heartbreaking in itself, but, when your children are forcibly taken away simply because you aren't seen as acceptable by society, even though you are the same person, the same parent you've always been ... that experience I can't even comprehend. It makes me look at my children and grandchildren with much greater appreciation for them than I had before becoming aware that some people can be forced from their kids and there's not a damn thing they can do about it.

My friend, Laura Perry, once posted on her Facebook page: "Some people are proud to be trans ... I just want to be female ... I was pretending to be a boy and now I'm pretending to be a girl ... there really isn't a place for me in this world ... all I've gone through, losing my wife, the money, the physical pain, the medical risks ... for what ... so I can pretend to be a girl? I was better at pretending to be a boy; at least I didn't have to look over my shoulder all the time."

Laura's post echoes the struggles of many transgender persons. So many times I wondered why in the world anyone would go through everything it takes to transition. Then my friend, Denise Johnson, made a comment during a conversation we had that gave me the answer to my questioning when she said, "My life is 1000 times harder than it ever has been, but I'm 1000 times happier than I've ever been." And isn't that the number one goal of every person ... happiness.

Be happy ... be yourself ... whoever you are ... and allow others to be themselves, whoever they are.

EPILOGUE

I'd dare say that when you, as the reader of this book, saw the pictures of me in Chapter 4 you may have drawn some conclusions as to how I *'was'* or how I *'am now'* based on my appearance in those pictures.

However, I am the same **ME** in both pictures. I have always been **ME** … and I will always be **ME**. Only my appearance changes. Unfortunately, I've spent much of my life being judged on my appearance, and I, myself, have been my most harsh judge.

It took me nearly two years to understand that as with me, the same goes for Alana … it is only appearance that has changed … and I initially jusdged her harshly based on a diference in appearance. But, I finally figured out that she is the same person she has always been, and will always be.

So, no matter what I saw in the past, or shall see in the future, the person is the same.